# WHERE on drugs

## a parents' handbook

## Edited by Beryl McAlhone

**Advisory Centre for Education**

We would like to thank all the many people who helped in the preparation of this booklet. In particular we are grateful to William Nash of the National Council for Civil Liberties, Dr Julia Dawkins of the Department of Health and Social Security, Admiral Caldwell of the Medical Council on Alcoholism, and Mr E. Carter and Dr A. B. Stewart of the Inner London Education Authority. We thank, too, all the others who gave us the benefit of their time and wisdom in helping to plan the booklet and their specialist advice in commenting on drafts.

© Advisory Centre for Education (ACE) Ltd
Printed in England by W. Heffer and Sons Ltd for ACE
SBN 900029 14 5 √

# Contents

# Contents

# Introduction

## BERYL McALHONE

*In the beginning, the way you get hooked in a lot of ways is because of this tremendous relief that you feel because of all these problems, anxieties and so forth becoming resolved all of a sudden. Here you've been worrying about them your whole life and they just get resolved all of a sudden, wham, like that. It isn't getting high, it's getting straightened out, you know, in a sense. Then, as you go along, that's when you begin to find out that horse is a cheat, a real cheap cheat – American girl.*

That comment by a heroin addict illustrates the major theme of this booklet: that there is no 'drugs problem', only problems which may get a 'drugs solution'.

It is perfectly natural for any parent to be concerned that a teenager might get caught up in a drugs way of life. But essentially that concern for an adolescent's well-being should be no more and no less than that of parents before the whole drugs problem arrived. For what is at stake is what has always been at stake: the capacity of a young person to go through the process of maturing without experiencing disabling stress. There have always been casualties: only today the casualties may be more noticeable, their tragedy more dramatic and abruptly terminated. But the children who come to grief with drugs are those in acute danger of catastrophe, anyway. Drugs simply provide a new version.

For, after all the efforts of research in the last few years into what *makes* a drug addict – why this or that boy or girl – the answer seems a plain one. As Dr D. V. Hawks, of the London Institute of Psychiatry Addiction Research Unit, puts it: 'It is perhaps simple-minded to imagine that the factors contributing to drug abuse are going to be different from those which contribute to other forms of social and personal pathology'.

### A new trap to fear?
Every parent who has seen a child unmistakably heading for trouble now has a new trap to fear. But every parent who has up till now watched the development of his children with a certain amount of content has no reason to feel any differently. That is not to say the adolescents concerned will never get 'involved' with drugs. Each and every one will probably try drugs or get the chance to try them before the age of 20. But what matters is the alternative satisfactions that are available. If life is good enough on its own, adolescents will, like some we talked to in preparing this booklet, take drugs or leave them.

But the teenager with the bleak inner life, with little he cares about, with minimal sources of satisfaction, may have nothing which rivals the stimulation of cannabis, or the sedation of barbiturates, so drugs could become his major preoccupation.

This booklet differs from some we have seen in that it places the drugs themselves slightly off-centre. For while it is essential to be well informed about them, too much emphasis on 'the drugs' by parents and adults concerned about dependence is no more than a mirror image of the addicts' approach. Just as an

1

addict may use the drug to cope with the *symptoms* – anxiety, loneliness, frustration – and not the *causes* of his predicament, so there is a corresponding danger that parents will focus exclusively on 'the drugs' rather than the problem behind them.

That is why a major section of this booklet is given over to a discussion of the various pitfalls of adolescence: the stresses that can arise from being legally an adult but still at school and within its rules; the tensions associated with career choice, and the winning of appropriate qualifications; the strains put on a developing personality by a school's unambiguous categorisation of 'success' and 'failure'; the search for personal style, in politics, dress, sex, and the parental conflict which is invariably involved. These are some of the 'presenting problems' of drug addiction, and the sensible parent will therefore be just as concerned about what goes on in the day-to-day routine of school as in the more flamboyant activities of the weekend.

### Rescue services: appalling neglect

We give, too, a breakdown of the facilities that exist for adolescents in trouble – whether it is 'drugs' trouble or not. And it is here that the real problem begins to emerge. For the whole framework of rescue services for anxious, disturbed or mentally-ill adolescents is an example of appalling neglect. At the last count there were just over 300 beds available in special adolescent psychiatric units – to satisfy a need which at the minimum could not be put lower than four times that total. In fact the most 'developed' institution to treat these cases is the approved school. Similarly, for less acute disturbance only university students can be said to be adequately looked after. Elsewhere there is no organised service at all, and what is being done is being done by voluntary bodies on their own initiative.

Those who have made the mental health of young people their special concern estimate that around 10 per cent of late adolescents will need treatment for slight or acute psychiatric disorder in any year. In towns where no facilities exist, that means one out of every 10 young people will either have the good luck to find a sympathetic adult who can advise and give support in a time of crisis, or will suffer stress unaided and may enter the downward spiral of deteriorating personality.

Drugs can severely compromise an adolescent's capacity to get on top of his troubles. Patterns of personal problem-solving established during adolescence are very significant in determining adult behaviour – so a boy who uses drugs to ward off reality prejudices his future ability to make an adequate adjustment to society. Such a boy may be called a drugs casualty – but he is really a casualty of the huge gap in our social services concerning the mental care of young people. The drugs scare will not have been totally negative if it draws attention to that lack.

*Beryl McAlhone became an educational journalist by chance after finishing a history degree at Bedford College, London, and has been editing WHERE for the past five years. In between issues of the magazine she has also edited separate publications on unstreaming in comprehensive schools, getting into university, girls' education, books for children, and career opportunities in the year 2000.*

# Facts about drugs

## A TABULATED GUIDE TO BASIC INFORMATION

The next section of this booklet is devoted to a breakdown of those facts about drugs that are of most importance to parents. Information is presented in a quasi-tabular form, so that comparisons can be made between drugs at a glance. Thus the 10 major questions concerning drug use are investigated in turn, and for each the basic information about the drugs is given. This grouping allows readers to check instantly how drugs compare in their capacity to induce dependence, in their harmful effects, in the extent of their control by the law, and so on.

For our comparison we have picked out the major drugs of abuse – amphetamines, barbiturates, LSD, cannabis, opiates, alcohol and tobacco – and included caffeine as a balancing substance. This categorisation follows the main lines of current drug dependence, but it is by no means comprehensive. Cocaine, for example, is not reported on except in so far as it is used in conjunction with heroin. Aeroplane glue, nutmeg, dry cleaning fluid, aspirin and cough mixtures are not included – though they can be and are misused. Similarly various sedative, tranquilliser and stimulant pills which do not fall into any of these groups may be misused. But the substances for which information is given in the following pages probably cover 95 per cent of current drug abuse.

The reports in each section are necessarily condensed, and in many areas the facts are by no means clearly established. It is not the purpose of this booklet to explore the byways of pharmacological controversy. The broad lines of current knowledge are established in the charts that follow, and readers who want to fill in some of the details here and there are guided to appropriate sources in the booklist at the end of the booklet.

The two major topics of 'addiction' and the 'spread of drug abuse' are, however, of such particular concern to parents that we have devoted further space for more detailed treatment in the later sections.

# 1—the drugs concerned: names,

## Amphetamines

A wide range of preparations of amphetamine are available in the UK, in tablets and capsules of various shapes, sizes and colours. The drug is a synthetic stimulant. Common substances include dexamphetamine (Dexedrine, 'dex' or 'dexies'), methylamphetamine (Methedrine), dextroamphetamine (Durophet, 'Black Bombers', 'Black and Tans') and phenmetrazine (Preludin). Also widely abused is the amphetamine/barbiturate compound Drinamyl, which changed its shape recently and consequently its name – from Purple Hearts to French Blues.

## Barbiturates

So called because of their derivation from barbituric acid, they are a depressant, or sedative, drug. Thirty or so preparations exist, mainly in the form of capsules or tablets of various colours, sizes and shapes. They differ in the onset and duration of their action. Phenobarbitone (Gardenal, Luminal) is long-acting and lasts 6 to 10 hours; amylobarbitone (Amytal) and butobarbitone (Soneryl) are intermediate acting and effective from 30 minutes up to a period of five or six hours; quinalbarbitone (Seconal) and pentobarbitone (Nembutal) are short-acting, with an onset of 15 minutes and duration of two or three hours. They are nicknamed goof-balls, barbs or sleepers.

## Tobacco

*Nicotiana tabacum* is grown in the North American continent, parts of Africa and the middle and far east. Its leaf is cured and prepared for smoking in cigars or cigarettes, or sometimes for chewing or sniffing.

## Alcohol

Alcohol is most commonly consumed as beer in Britain. £837 million was spent on it in 1965, compared with £580 million spent on wines and spirits. It is one of the sedative and hypnotic drugs. Methanol (meths) is also drunk, but usually only by the more desperate addicts.

# nicknames, appearance

## LSD

D-lysergic acid diethylamide (LSD 25) is a synthethic hallucinogenic (or psychotomimetic or psychedelic) drug. It is available as a colourless, tasteless, odourless liquid, or an off-white powder, or a small white pill. Slang names for it include acid, instant zen, hawk, chief and sugar. Recently LSD appeared in capsule form, known as cherry top, purple haze or blue cheer.

## Cannabis

Pot comes from the flowering tops and leaves of the Indian hemp plant (*cannabis sativa* or *indica*), grown in many hot countries. 'Official' names, according to region and the plant product, are ganja, charas, bangh, kif and maconha. Users call it grass, pot, hash, tea, weed, charge, loco-weed, griefo, hay, hemp, jive, Mary Jane, mezz, rope, Texas tea, and many other things. It is available as crushed plant (marihuana), a cube of resin (hashish) or a brown powder. The drug belongs to the family of hallucinogens.

## Caffeine

Caffeine is a stimulant found in tea, coffee and cocoa. An average cup of tea contains up to 65 mg of caffeine, coffee up to 250 mg.

## Opiates

The opium poppy is the source of the hard-core narcotic drugs – opium and its derivatives, morphine, codeine and heroin. Synthetic narcotics are pethidine and methadone. All are powerful analgesics (painkillers). Heroin, the major drug of abuse, is available here in the form of tiny white pills, about the size of synthetic sweeteners, containing $\frac{1}{6}$ grain. Nicknames are, variously, H, horse, boy, harry, jack, joy powder, kick, junk, dope, scat, schmee, schmeck, shit.

# 2—how the drug is taken

**Amphetamines**
Almost invariably swallowed in tablet form. Methedrine was once available in liquid form for injecting, but supplies are now entirely restricted to hospitals.

**Barbiturates**
Usually taken orally in tablet or capsule form, but a recent practice has been to dissolve the tablet or capsule in water and inject.

**Tobacco**
Usually inhaled as smoke in the form of cigarettes. Or smoked without inhalation in the form of cigar or pipe tobacco. Less commonly it is chewed, or in powder form sniffed.

**Alcohol**
The drug is taken in various strengths and forms in the following drinks:

| | |
|---|---|
| ginger beer | 1 – 3 per cent alcohol |
| ale, beer, cider | 2 – 8 per cent alcohol |
| wine | 10 – 15 per cent alcohol |
| sherry, port | 20 per cent alcohol |
| liqueurs, spirits | 40 –50 per cent alcohol |

Poly drug users occasionally inject alcohol.

## LSD

A drop of the drug in liquid form is taken on a sugar cube, a piece of blotting or cigarette paper, licked off a stamp, or diluted in liquid and drunk. LSD is also available in capsule and tablet form.

## Cannabis

Cannabis resin can be eaten incorporated into sweetmeats or cakes; crushed up it can be put into a 'soft-drink'; most commonly it is smoked, either in a pipe or a specially rolled cigarette – a 'joint' or 'stick' or 'spliff' or 'reefer'.

## Caffeine

Drunk in tea, coffee or cocoa.

## Opiates

Heroin can be taken orally in tablet form, but users who want more immediate results generally prefer injection – either under the skin (skin popping), into a muscle, or into a vein (mainlining). Heroin can also be inhaled or sniffed. It is frequently injected or sniffed together with cocaine, a powerful stimulant, which counters its sedative effects. Methadone is usually taken orally.

# 3—effects of the drug; what an

**Amphetamines**
Their effect is to stimulate the central nervous system. The circulation of blood will be increased, stimulating the brain and alerting the senses. Appetite is decreased and fatigue warded off. The user is probably talkative, excited, elated. Heavy use will produce a prolonged state of wakefulness, sometimes truculent and aggressive behaviour, irritability and paranoia. The user may have dilated pupils, and experience shaking hands and profuse perspiration.

**Barbiturates**
The effect of their progressive depression of the brain's activity ranges from mild sedation to coma. Early effects of a large dose resemble drunkenness, with dilatation of pupils, sluggishness, slow thought and slurred speech, slow respiration, inaccurate judgement and reduced inhibitions. Some may exhibit irritability, paranoia, even suicidal tendencies. Sleep follows; at a high dose the sleep is very deep with depression of respiration and blood pressure.

**Tobacco**
Tobacco has variable effects on bodily function. It may cause constriction of certain blood vessels, and irritates the linings of the bronchial tract. It may either stimulate or sedate the brain.

**Alcohol**
The effects of alcohol are to increase the flow of gastric juices, stimulate the heart, inhibit appetite, depress the central nervous system, dilate blood vessels, causing loss of body heat, and increase the flow of urine. Visual signs are excited, then slurred speech, irresponsible actions, increased self-confidence, loss of body balance. The user suffers some disturbance of cerebral function.

# observer will notice

## LSD

Heart rate and blood pressure are increased. Some experience dilatation of pupils, variation in blood sugar levels, shaking of hands and feet, cold sweaty palms, flushed face, shivering chills, nausea and loss of appetite. The subjective effects are unpredictable and vary with individuals and occasions. The 'trip' begins within 30 minutes to an hour and lasts anything from four to 10 hours, with strong and bizarre mental reactions and distortion in physical senses. Users can experience hallucinatory phenomena with vivid enjoyment or acute anxiety and distress. Emotional repressions may be broken down and memories and experiences released from the unconscious.

## Cannabis

The variation in effect on individuals is greater with cannabis than with any other drug. Commonly it causes a quickening of the heart beat, a fluctuation in the level of blood sugar and a drop in body temperature. Dilatation of the pupils, reddening of the eyes, increased appetite, a craving for sugar and an urge to urinate sometimes occur. Users may experience dizziness, a dry throat, nausea and vomiting. The drug can remove inhibition, slightly impair judgement and memory, distort perception and sensation and increase sexual desire. Mood changes may be in the direction of inconsequential hilarity, excitement, euphoria and loquaciousness, or alternatively depression, apprehension, even panic. The effects begin within minutes of smoking and last up to four hours, according to dose.

## Caffeine

As a result of the action of caffeine on the cortex, a person becomes less tired and more alert; his thinking appears to be more precise and there is a reduction in his reaction time. When large doses are taken, the stimulation of the central nervous system is succeeded by depression.

## Opiates

In its depression of the central nervous system, heroin offers the most powerful relief available for physical and mental pain. This is accompanied by a fair degree of sedation. Initial use can cause nausea and vomiting, but this will later be replaced by the feeling of 'high' – a deeply experienced pleasure. This 'buzz' or 'flash' follows quickly on injection, but the effect subsides during months of use and then disappears. Other effects are depression of the respiratory system, an inhibition of the stomach and intestinal muscles, and a reduction of hunger, thirst and the sex drive. Observers can notice pin-point pupils, and the early display of sleepy well-being, which changes to restlessness and anxiety as the time for another 'fix' approaches. Other signs are scars and bruises in the injection area and blood spots.

9

# 4—source of supply; cost

**Amphetamines**
The drug has been widely prescribed: the re-selling of over-prescribed pills and thefts from chemists' shops create the illicit supply. An Ipswich experiment of imposing a voluntary ban on prescribing has cut back illicit use very severely.

The cost of a tablet may range from 1s to 7s 6d (the retail value of Durophet is 6s a 100).

**Barbiturates**
Available on prescription by a doctor. Illicit supplies are fed by thefts from chemists' shops and over-prescription.

The black market cost is variable, depending on availability: approximately 2s 6d a tablet.

**Tobacco**
Open access, but it is a contravention of the law to sell tobacco to children under the age of 16. However, a serious problem is posed by the impossibility of preventing children from using vending machines.

The cost of a cigarette is around 3d but varies as much as 90 per cent with brand.

**Alcohol**
Open access, except for licensing hours regulations.

Alcohol can be bought for upwards of 1s 6d: approximately £1 buys an intoxicating amount.

| | |
|---|---|
| **LSD**<br>All supplies are illicit.<br><br>The cost is around 20s – 30s a dose. | **Cannabis**<br>All supplies are illicit.<br><br>£1 buys a lump of resin (hashish) half the size of a sugar cube. Altogether one ounce of resin costs about £12 and is enough for about 50 joints – more than a month's supply for even a comparatively heavy user. |
| **Caffeine**<br>Access is open.<br>Cost is minimal. | **Opiates**<br>The only legal supplies of heroin are those prescribed by doctors working at the specially designated treatment units in the UK. Methadone is prescribable in the normal way.<br><br>The cost of heroin on the black market is around £4 – £6 a grain, depending on availability. The black market is, however, very small. |

# 5—medical use and safe dosages

## Amphetamines

Medical use has been widespread as an appetite suppressant, to maintain wakefulness, to increase endurance and as an anti-depressant. Probably only in the treatment of narcolepsy, however, will these substances be used in areas where doctors wish to restrict supplies.

Tolerance develops to the drug, so that heavy users may build up to a dose of 20 – 30 pills a day. The clinical dose is 5 mg (1 tablet) three times a day.

## Barbiturates

The major medical use is to produce sedation. Also used in the treatment of epilepsy and, in the case of the extremely short-acting barbiturates, as an intravenous anaesthetic.

The clinical dose of phenobarbitone is 100 mg. An individual who has acquired tolerance to the drug can take as much as 10 $\times$ 100 mg in 24 hours.

## Tobacco

No medical use.

Present knowledge suggests that there is a risk of damage to health to any smoker, and that even one cigarette a day is not safe. The risk, however, increases markedly over the limit of 10 to 15 a day.

## Alcohol

Used medically only as a disinfectant, to dilate peripheral blood vessels and as a mild sedative for the elderly.

Toxic symptoms are produced by 16 – 25 grams circulating in the blood. A blood concentration of 0.2 per cent usually causes drunkenness. 80 milligrams of alcohol per 100 millilitres of blood is set as the intake for drivers. 450 mg/100 ml blood content constitutes acute poisoning.

## LSD

Some doctors believe it has potential value in the treatment of psychiatric disorders, but results from this kind of use have been inconsistent.

The doses are so small, they are measured in microgrammes – a thousandth of a milligram. The minimal effective dose is 20 – 30 microgrammes. The optimum dose is between 100 microgrammes and 1 milligram. Larger doses are not toxic, though the effects are not pleasant.

## Cannabis

No medical uses.

Its effects are felt with the first cigarette. Depending on the quality of the marihuana, roughly four will bring changes in perception. After 10 cigarettes hallucinations and illusions may occur, plus great joy, or deep unease, fear and panic. Experienced users can regulate their intake so as not to go beyond the desired levels. Most will smoke only one or two cigarettes on each occasion.

## Caffeine

Used occasionally as a stimulant.

65 to 300 mg constitutes the recommended medicinal dose. Over 600 mg constitutes a toxic dose.

## Opiates

Used medically as the most powerful of all pain killers: morphine is used in treating accident injuries, heart disease and post-operative pain; heroin for incurable diseases. The clinical dose is half a tablet ($\frac{1}{12}$ grain) but users soon exceed this. Mild symptoms are precipitated by 20 – 30 mg ($\frac{1}{3}$ to $\frac{1}{2}$ grain), serious symptoms by 100 mg ($1\frac{2}{3}$ grain). As tolerance develops, addicts increase the dose until they may be taking two dozen tablets (four grains) a day – a fatal dose for a normal person.

13

# 6—side-effects of the drug, and

**Amphetamines**
Minor side-effects include dry mouth, restlessness, insomnia, headaches, dizziness and tremor. An overdose of 50 to 60 tablets can produce hallucinations, delusions of persecution and psychosis ('the horrors'). The 'come-down' following use brings extreme fatigue and mental depression.

**Tobacco**
Tobacco smoke causes changes, eventually irreversible, in the tissues of the respiratory tract, and mouth, and damage to the heart and blood vessels. Chronic bronchitis and emphysema can be produced by the repeated irritation of the respiratory system. Heavy cigarette smoking in particular can induce malignant changes that lead to cancer of the lung. Altogether a minimum of 75,000 deaths each year are attributed to the effects of smoking. Approximately 10 per cent of all premature deaths are due to smokers' diseases. A further large, but unknown, number of people are incapacitated by bronchitis. It is estimated that one million men and women will die in Britain in this decade as a result of smoking cigarettes.

**Barbiturates**
Driving under the influence of barbiturates is dangerous, as is the potentiation of the drug by mixing it with alcohol or morphine. The habit of injecting barbiturates is extremely hazardous: impurities in the drug may lead to sores and abscesses which refuse to heal, gangrenous limbs, ulcerated hands and feet, the necessity for amputation of a limb, even death. The drug is popular too, for suicide attempts. Two thousand people die each year from barbiturate poisoning: 16,000 are admitted to hospital with this condition – a total of 2 per cent of all admissions. Death may be caused by the depression of respiration, collapse of the circulatory system, or inhalation of vomit. A user may survive coma but suffer irreparable brain damage caused by the deprivation of oxygen.

**Alcohol**
Prolonged, heavy use of alcohol can lead to social deterioration, malnutrition, gastritis and peptic ulcer, neuritis, cirrhosis, psychosis and even epileptiform convulsions. A particular bout of drinking may end in coma. Death may occur following inhalation of vomit. Methanol causes severe abdominal pain, acidosis and disturbance, even loss, of vision.

# how it harms the user

**LSD**
Since the effect of the drug is unpredictable, some experience deep distress. Others panic at being unable to stop its action. It can build up a paranoic state which may persist for several days. Under its influence accidental deaths have followed a user's disturbed interpretation of reality. Hallucinations may recur weeks later, causing the user to fear insanity.

**Cannabis**
Unwanted side effects of cannabis may be lethargy, inertia and self-neglect. The user may be deluded by false feelings of increased capability, with consequent disappointments. Some react adversely to the drug and may experience panic and anxiety.

**Caffeine**
Anyone with a peptic ulcer may find caffeine harmful. Fatalities following the misuse of caffeine are extremely rare, except where strong coffee might be drunk by someone with a weak heart. Some cases of chronic poisoning have occurred in Scandinavian countries where coffee consumption is high.

**Opiates**
Unwanted side effects of heroin use are constipation and cessation of menstruation. Addicts are vulnerable to infections and liver damage through using unsterile needles, and embolism from injecting air into a vein. An overdose can lead to respiratory failure. Addiction carries a high death risk – a mortality rate 20 – 35 times the normal. The 69 deaths during 1965–6 were at a mean age of 24.8 years, caused as follows:

| | |
|---|---|
| suicide | 9 |
| suicidal overdose | 7 |
| accidental overdose | 16 |
| sudden death | 4 |
| violent death | 6 |
| septic conditions | 15 |
| other | 12 |

# 7—is there a risk of dependence?

## Amphetamines

It is estimated that one fifth of the women and a quarter of the men who regularly use amphetamine will become habituated. The World Health Organisation defines it as a drug of psychological rather than physical dependence. As tolerance develops so does the need to increase the dose.

## Barbiturates

The World Health Organisation has described barbiturates as drugs of dependence on account of:

1 – the craving to continue taking the drug.

2 – the tendency to increase the dose as tolerance is established.

3 – psychic dependence on the effects of the drug.

4 – physical dependence, creating an abstinence syndrome if the drug is withdrawn.

An estimated one sixth of all regular users are dependent.

## Tobacco

The majority of people who smoke to any extent at all become dependent, and only a minority of smokers succeed in relinquishing the habit. Cigarette smokers who are unable to give up can switch to the less dangerous habit of cigar or pipe smoking. Dependence is complex: partly social, partly psychological and to an extent pharmacological.

## Alcohol

It is estimated that one in 150 of alcohol users are physically dependent, and a much larger number psychologically dependent. Tolerance develops so that the user progressively increases the dose.

## LSD

LSD is not physically addicting. There is no development of tolerance, but repeated use leads to diminished effects, which can only be re-established with the passage of time. Confirmed users may still only take it two or three times a week.

## Cannabis

The World Health Organisation has recognised cannabis as a drug of psychological dependence, with the following characteristics:

1 – its subjective effects can stimulate desire for the drug.

2 – there is little or no development of tolerance of the drug and consequently little or no tendency to increase the dose.

3 – it creates no physical dependence so there is no abstinence syndrome when it is discontinued.

4 – the dependence is psychic, based on subjective and individual appreciation of the drug's effects.

## Caffeine

Some psychic dependence is postulated.

## Opiates

Heroin is the classic drug of physical dependence, though users would need to take it repeatedly over a short period of time for this dependence to develop. Drug dependence of the morphine type is characterised by an overpowering desire or need to continue with the drug, an increase in dosage as tolerance develops, psychic dependence based on subjective appreciation of the drug's effects and physical dependence for the maintenance of homeostasis – an abstinence syndrome develops when the drug is withdrawn.

# 8—when the drug is withdrawn:

**Amphetamines**
There is no withdrawal syndrome. However, the 'come-down' after heavy use involves physical exhaustion, extreme depression and a state of anxiety.

**Barbiturates**
Withdrawal symptoms start within 12 hours of taking the drug, reach peak intensity in two or three days, and subside after about a week. Early effects are anxiety, twitching, shaking, weakness, dizziness, distorted vision, nausea, vomiting, insomnia, weight loss and loss in blood pressure on standing. A user at the level of 900 mg a day will probably then suffer epileptic fits, delirium, hallucinations of a persecutory nature and suicidal tendencies. Withdrawal of barbiturates in fact is more dangerous than heroin withdrawal, and can produce death. An additional dose of the drug in this case will not relieve all the symptoms.

**Tobacco**
Symptoms are very variable: some people have physical symptoms, others anxiety, depression and intense craving. The symptoms fade in a matter of weeks.

**Alcohol**
Withdrawal of alcohol causes marked anxiety, restlessness, confusion, tremulousness, fever and, after very heavy use, delirium tremens. Convulsions and death may follow.

# physical consequences

**LSD**
No abstinence syndrome when the drug is withdrawn.

**Cannabis**
No abstinence syndrome when the drug is withdrawn.

**Caffeine**
Total withdrawal of caffeine after heavy use may produce a headache.

**Opiates**
Withdrawal symptoms begin within about four hours of taking the drug and rise to a peak after 18 hours. If untreated they subside by the sixth or seventh day.

Slight symptoms are those of running eyes and nose, aches, dilated pupils, yawning, apprehension, restlessness, hot and cold flushes and gooseflesh. The more severe symptoms create a personal hell of fever, loss of appetite, weight loss, dehydration, sleeplessness, prolific perspiration, nausea, vomiting, cramps, diarrhoea and sharp pain in limbs.

# 9—drug users and abusers

## Amphetamines

Once widely prescribed as a pick-me-up and slimming pill for housewives, an estimated 500 out of Newcastle's population of 270,000 were dependent on it in the early sixties. Estimates made by Dr Thomas Bewley in 1966 give the following figures for misuse of amphetamines (and other substances covered here): 100–200 per 100,000 population have slight dependence on prescribed amphetamines. A further 100–200 per 100,000 use it illicitly.

**Summary of misuse**
## 300 per 100,000

## Barbiturates

About two per cent of the total population regularly take barbiturates. This drug makes up 7 per cent of all National Health Service prescriptions. Approximately 150–200 per 100,000 population are physically dependent on it; 800–1,200 per 100,000 use it regularly, with probable psychic dependence.

**Summary of misuse**
## 1,200 per 100,000

## Tobacco

Altogether 42 per cent of women in Britain and 67 per cent of men smoke. The numbers are increasing in the younger age groups, and falling in the older age groups.

**Summary of misuse**
## 42,000 per 100,000

## Alcohol

An estimated 75 per cent of the population uses alcohol. It is estimated that 140 in 100,000 are obvious and chronic alcoholics; 400 in 100,000 are alcoholics showing signs of early physical and mental deterioration; and a further 120 in 100,000 are physically dependent on the drug.

**Summary of misuse**
## 660 per 100,000

**LSD**
Approximately less than 5 in 100,000 are estimated to use LSD in the UK.

**Cannabis**
An estimated 30–60 per 100,000 regularly use cannabis in the UK. The yearly total for cannabis offences has gone up from less than a hundred in 1957 to 5,287 in 1968. The United States National Institute of Mental Health estimates that of all users:
65 per cent only experiment, using it just 1 – 10 times;
25 per cent are occasional, social users;
10 per cent are chronic users, devoting a significant amount of time to the drug. The Association for the Prevention of Addiction estimates from its experience that only 5 per cent of cannabis users escalate to hard drugs.

**Summary of misuse**
up to 5 per 100,000

**Summary of misuse**
45 per 100,000

**Caffeine**
Approximately 95,000 per 100,000 use caffeine.

**Opiates**
The 1969 figure for known addicts is 2,881 in the UK: five per 100,000 population. Numbers were doubling roughly every 18 months between 1964 and 1968; but the rate has since slowed down. Since the 1968 legislation the number of 'registered' addicts has probably been a better guide to the real total than it was before.

**Summary of misuse**
nil

**Summary of misuse**
5 per 100,000

# 10—drugs and the law

## Amphetamines

Under the 1964 Drugs (Prevention of Misuse) Act it is an offence to be in unauthorised possession of amphetamines. Existing penalties are, on indictment, up to two years in prison and/or an unspecified fine, and on summary conviction six months in prison and/or a £200 fine. Legislation being prepared introduces two new distinctions, between penalties for 'pushers' and those in possession, and between injectable and other amphetamines. 'Pushing' in either case would carry a penalty on indictment of up to 14 years' imprisonment and/or an unlimited fine; possession of *injectable* amphetamines would carry a maximum penalty of seven years; possession of *non-injectable* amphetamines would carry five years, and/or an unlimited fine in both cases (lower penalties on summary conviction).

## Barbiturates

Under the Pharmacy and Poisons Act 1933 barbiturates are not sold openly and must be obtained on prescription. Sale must be supervised by a registered pharmacist, and entered in the poisons book. The drugs do not figure in the Dangerous Drugs Acts, though current investigations may result in this being changed.

## Tobacco

There are few restrictions on the sale or use of tobacco. Cigarette advertisements are no longer permitted on TV, and under the Children and Young Persons Act 1933, the sale of cigarettes and other forms of tobacco is forbidden to children under 16. This is triable summarily, and carries a penalty of a £25 fine on first conviction, £50 fine on second conviction and £100 on third or subsequent convictions. However, the law is exceedingly difficult to enforce because of the use of vending machines.

## Alcohol

The Licensing Acts restrict the hours when alcohol is on sale, and limit that sale to people aged 18 or over. Under the Road Traffic Acts 1960–62 and the Road Safety Act 1967, people driving under the influence of drink face disqualification from driving for at least a year, and penalties on indictment of an unlimited fine and/or two years' imprisonment, and on summary conviction £100 and/or four months' imprisonment (rising to six months on second conviction). It is also an offence to fail to provide a breath sample (punishable summarily by a fine of £50) or a blood or urine sample if the breath test is positive (which is punishable as if it were the principal offence).

## LSD
Under the 1964 Drugs (Prevention of Misuse) Act it is an offence to be in unauthorised possession of LSD.

Existing penalties are up to two years in prison and/or an unlimited fine on indictment (£200 and/or six months on summary conviction). Under the proposed legislation LSD would be grouped with heroin and attract the severest penalties for trafficking and supplying (up to 14 years in prison and/or an unlimited fine on indictment; £400 and/or 12 months on summary conviction) and for possession (up to 7 years and/or an unlimited fine on indictment; £400 and/or 12 months on summary conviction).

## Cannabis
Under the Dangerous Drugs Act 1965 both possession, and trafficking and smuggling are punishable by a fine of up to £1,000 and 10 years in prison on indictment (£250 and/or 12 months on summary conviction). The new legislation would reduce the maximum prison sentence on indictment for possession to five years, and increase that for trafficking and smuggling to 14 years. Fines in both instances would be unlimited (summary conviction in both cases: £400 and/or 12 months). The police have powers of arrest and search of those suspected of unlawful possession.

## Caffeine
No regulations.

## Opiates
Raw and prepared opium and their derivatives are strictly controlled by law – both in manufacture and supply. The prescribing of heroin is limited to specified doctors working in a selected number of psychiatric hospitals throughout the country and in the 15 special treatment centres in London. Unlawful supply and possession currently carry penalties of £1,000 or 10 years' imprisonment on indictment; £250 and/or 12 months on summary conviction. The new legislation would change that to 14 years for trafficking and 7 years for possession, both with unlimited fines, on indictment; £400 and/or 12 months on summary conviction.

# More about the law of dangerous drugs

Some very important provisions of the law relate to the powers of the police of search and arrest. Under the 1964 Act a constable may arrest anybody without warrant if he finds him committing, or reasonably suspects him of having committed, an offence under the Drugs Acts, with the condition that the constable believes

1 – he will abscond unless arrested;

2 – his name and address are unknown and unascertainable;

3 – he is not satisfied the name and address furnished are correct.

These powers are subject to the ill-defined test of 'reasonableness'.

Under the Dangerous Drugs Act 1967 a warrant may be issued to search specific premises whenever and as often as required within a month of its issue. Under the same Act a policeman may search anyone without arrest or warrant, in the street if necessary, subject to a similar test of 'reasonable suspicion'.

Under the 1965 Act, trial on indictment (that is before a judge and jury) is not permitted without the consent of the Attorney-General or the Director of Public Prosecutions (under the Misuse of Drugs Bill only the consent of the DPP will be required). Thus the more usual practice is appearance before a magistrate (on summary conviction) and the maximum penalties (especially for first offenders) are thus the lighter ones.

It is also possible for the owner or occupier of premises to be charged for allowing drugs to be consumed on his premises under the 1965 Act. However, since the decision in Sweet v Parsley this is no longer regarded as an 'absolute' offence and it must be proved that the owner/occupier had knowledge of the incident.

The Misuse of Drugs Bill (which is still going through Parliament and may therefore be amended) does not substantially change the law of search in its present form. It creates offences of trafficking, and imposes a category system of drugs according to harmfulness. Three classes are envisaged: class A (including opiates and LSD); class B (including amphetamines, Drinamyl and cannabis); and class C (less harmful drugs, mainly amphetamine-type). The penalties, and occasionally the offences, will vary according to category. The legislation is intended to be flexible so that drugs can be added or moved into a different category as circumstances change.

# What is addiction?

## NEHKANT RATHOD

Excessive use of chemicals is not unique to any particular society, although it is true that the type of chemicals used may vary from community to community, and within the same community from time to time. For example, alcohol, hypnotics and amphetamines are more widely mis-used in materially affluent communities like those of the West than are opiates and cannabis, which find favour among the materially not so developed countries of south-east Asia and the Middle East. None the less noticeable use of the opiates and hallucinogenic drugs like cannabis or LSD has developed in the last 10 years in the United Kingdom.

It appears that mis-use of chemicals is a particular attribute of human beings, and past experience suggests that the mis-use will continue, with perhaps more and more new chemicals being available for this purpose.

In such a situation it is important that we learn about some of the basic issues relating to drug abuse, for two reasons – one being that social vigilance and individual effort is necessary if the number of mis-users is to be kept to the minimum that a society can afford; the second being that dogmatic opinions and attitudes based predominantly on ignorance can and do lead to a kind of witch-hunt.

What is a drug? Briefly, a drug is any chemical (or biological substance), natural or synthetic, which is prescribed, or administered without prescription, to diagnose, treat, or prevent ill-health, however caused.

The drugs which presently concern us are those likely to produce 'dependence'. An interesting quality shared by most of these drugs is their obvious effects on the nervous system – specifically the brain. They alter more than one of the following three areas of brain activity: intellectual processes, mood (emotions or feelings), and perceptual activity. For example, alcohol predominately affects the higher and finer intellectual functions (for example, inhibitions, co-ordination, judgement). Barbiturates primarily affect the level of consciousness (awareness, and sensitivity to environment). Amphetamines principally elevate mood, bring about a feeling of euphoria and, associated with it, increased activity. Hallucinogens, like cannabis and much more so LSD, bring about both qualitative and quantitative changes in one's perception. Opiates (morphine, heroin and physeptone, alias methadone) primarily abolish or dull perception of pain – including psychological suffering or pain.

### What is abuse?

Abuse can be said to occur in the following circumstances:

1 – Use of drugs proscribed by law constitutes abuse. This may be administration of a drug which has not been prescribed (heroin, say) or administration of drugs which are (for all practical purposes) illegal to possess (for example, cannabis).

2 – The second form of abuse is where the community we live in or like to belong to does not tolerate or frowns on the use of a particular drug (as with alcohol or tobacco in some religious sects). Users are consequently looked on as deviants.

25

3 – The third type of abuse is excessive use, which endangers one's own health or disturbs social harmony.

One can therefore understand why smoking even one cigarette of cannabis can lead to the humiliation of a Court appearance, to being deprived of one's liberty as a citizen, to being expelled from school and thus having one's future put into jeopardy. Yet no one has proved that occasional cannabis smoking leads to physical or social harm, or inevitably to addiction or dependence. So it is very difficult to see the validity of any rationale underlying such attitudes.

Addiction is a omnibus term which does not really define addiction, but describes an addict. It is gradually being replaced by the term 'dependence', although the term 'addiction' remains engrained in social vocabulary.

## Drug dependence: an official definition

In 1964 the World Health Organisation Expert Committee proposed abandoning the term 'addiction' to be replaced by the term 'dependence'. Five types of dependence were recognised – each with different characteristics. They concerned 1 – morphine and its analogues, 2 – barbiturates, 3 – cocaine, 4 – amphetamines and 5 – cannabis. All these drugs are classed as narcotics. Alcohol was not in their terms of reference.

These were the characteristics the World Health Organisation included in its definitions.

1 – whether or not there is a strong desire or need for the drug;

2 – whether or not the user acquires 'tolerance' to the drug and therefore needs to increase the dose;

3 – whether or not there is pyschic dependence on the effects of the drug related to subjective and individual appreciation of those effects;

4 – whether or not there is physical dependence on the drug, so that its presence is required for the maintenance of homeostasis, and an abstinence syndrome develops.

The following table summarises the World Health Organisation definitions of the characteristics of each of these five drugs of dependence.

|  | heroin | barbitur- ates | cocaine | amphet- amines | cannabis |
|---|---|---|---|---|---|
| Need for drugs | yes | yes | yes | yes | yes |
| Tolerance | yes | yes | yes | yes | no(?) |
| Psychic dependence | yes | yes | yes | yes | yes |
| Physical dependence | yes | yes | no | no | no |

These definitions may well be rewritten as further work is done on the question of dependence, in particular the definition of a psychological withdrawal syndrome in addition to the physical withdrawal syndrome.

The important thing about the WHO definitions is that they stipulate that dependence may be psychological and/or physical. The degree of psychological dependence is difficult to assess, as its main criterion is patients' subjective feelings

26

from the drugs. These are often exaggerated. However, psychological dependence is marked in amphetamine and tobacco users. Alcohol, barbiturates and opiate-dependent people will show both types of dependence when the drug is withheld.

This discussion tells us what drug dependence is but not much of the mechanisms of how dependence is produced. Evidence derived from experiments on animals and humans is just beginning to give some answers.

The following is an attempt to paraphrase the findings on the development of 'tolerance'. The nerve cells of the body are in constant activity of one sort or another and are emitting impulses. The drugs in question (say heroin or barbiturates) put up an artificial dam or block and thus stop the flow of impulses. This results in the desired action of the drug – to block pain, or to block a state of being awake or restless. As time goes on the nerve cells can partially overcome this block or dam – thus diminishing the effectiveness of the drug. So more drug is needed to achieve the desired effect, to dam the flow of impulses. This is how tolerance develops.

Now imagine the drug being suddenly withdrawn, that is, withheld from the user. The whole system will be flooded by the impulses so far blocked by drugs (that is, by the chemicals which transmit the impulses) and this is what leads to the withdrawal or the abstinence syndrome. Here also lies the explanation of why people have to use the drug repeatedly and more or less continuously. This is because most of the drugs mentioned are active only for a short time and as soon as they are metabolised or excreted, the supply to the tissues needs to be replenished to avoid the abstinence syndrome. This compares well with clinical experience that initially people take these drugs for their positive effects, but with the passing months or years they come to realise that although they do not get the desired effect, they still have to take the drug – now primarily to avoid the withdrawal or abstinence syndrome.

**What makes a user dependent?**
To produce dependence repeated or continued use of a drug over a period (weeks in the case of opiates, months in the case of barbiturates, and years in the case of alcohol), is required. In other words, very occasional use does not lead to dependence. It is true that dependence is impossible among those who never taste alcohol. It is also true that the possibility of dependence on alcohol increases if you start using alcohol. But it is interesting that not more than one or two per cent of the drinking population becomes dependent, this despite the fact that a sizeable percentage have occasionally used alcohol excessively, to their own detriment or the discomfort of others.

As far as abuse of heroin or other opiates is concerned, the chances of becoming dependent are greater than with alcohol or barbiturates, but there are no controlled studies to prove this, and none seem ethically possible.

Clinical experience suggests, however, that while occasional use of opiates can lead to dependence more readily than with other drugs, none the less, many of the youngsters who try heroin, even by injection, do so on a once only basis, or on a once or twice a week basis and never go any further. In other words, use is not synonymous with addiction except in the eyes of the ignorant or the prejudiced; and if this is true for heroin, the most potentially addicting drug of all, it is even more true for other drugs.

We can summarise the information on dependence for the main drugs covered by this pamphlet in the table overleaf.

| Criteria of Dependence | tobacco | alcohol | barbiturates | amphetamines | cannabis | opiates (heroin physeptone) | LSD |
|---|---|---|---|---|---|---|---|
| 'irresistible' desire | yes | yes | yes | yes | yes | yes | yes |
| increased tolerance | yes | yes | yes | yes | no(?) | yes | no |
| psychological dependence | yes | yes | yes | yes | yes | yes | yes |
| physical dependence | not proven | yes | yes | not proven | not proven | yes | not proven |
| average period between regular use and development of dependence | ? | months or years | months | weeks | months | weeks | ? |
| usual age of dependent person | teenage and adults | adults | adults | teenage and adults | teenage | teenage | teenage and adults |
| physical withdrawal syndrome | no | yes | yes | no | no | yes | no |
| characteristics | – | delirium tremens | convulsions | – | – | autonomic disturbance | – |
| psychological withdrawal syndrome | yes | yes | yes | yes | yes | yes | yes |
| characteristics | inability to relax | inability to relax and concentrate. Depression | as for alcohol | as for alcohol | as for alcohol | as for alcohol | as for alcohol |

Even though parents may recognise that they have little to fear from their children using a not-particularly-addicting drug, they may be concerned about escalation – that use of a so-called 'soft drug' will lead to use of a so-called 'hard drug'.

The criteria of what constitutes soft or hard drugs have never been formulated. I suppose cannabis, amphetamines and barbiturates fall into the former category: heroin into the latter. The myth of escalation arises from arguing backwards. It is true that most people who are dependent on heroin have used or do use the other so-called soft drugs, but this is not the same as saying that all or most people who use the so-called soft drugs will go on to hard drugs. At least we have not been able to confirm this trend. This fallacy is often overlooked. It is perhaps worth recording that sometimes the so-called soft drugs (barbiturates and amphetamines, for example) can be very crippling and socially damaging. Thus although escalation remains a deceptive concept, people may (but not necessarily) move from one class of drugs to another.

A second myth is that drug abuse leads to crime. This depends on what one assumes is crime. In strictly legal terms many drug abusers are criminal because they act against the law of the land by consuming a proscribed drug. If one excludes the minority of drug dependent people who have alienated themselves from society or have been rejected by the family and society, our local experience suggests that cannabis and heroin, if anything, neutralise acquisitiveness and violent crimes. The same, however, may not be said of users of amphetamines and alcohol, and of abusers generally who have been criminally habituated before starting drug abuse or who have to commit crime to finance their drug supply, as happens in the United States.

## How dependence develops

For dependence to develop you require the drug, the user and the environment. Those three interact with each other in ways which, by and large, still remain a mystery. The one tangible and identifiable aspect is 'the drug', and therefore a good deal of emphasis has been placed, and justly so, on reducing or stamping out the availability of the drug. This is also the easier of the three aspects to counter. However, one should bear in mind the danger that we may be ignoring: the two other aspects of drug dependence, the user and the environment.

If you take the analogy of an uprising, drugs are like weapons. Weapons are a means used by those involved in the uprising. Their banning and confiscation may be necessary as an expedient, as a short term measure to quell an uprising. But depriving people of the means of uprising does not stop festering discontent; and as long as this remains misunderstood and untackled, this discontent is very likely to lead to another uprising, although the weapons used (other drugs or other means) may be different next time.

The drug, then, may be much less important than the motivation of the taker. But the exact role of personality and circumstance in leading to drug dependence is still little understood, partly, and only partly, because the problem has not been with us long enough for us to gather experience and expertise.

The majority of drug users come from seemingly conforming, law-abiding and socially stable families. Our local experience, by no means representative of the country as a whole, suggests that a significant minority of these people had encountered a rather adverse emotional upbringing. Adults in these people's families have presented the children with examples of maladaptive and non-conforming behaviour in the nature of prolonged and severe discord between the parents. There has been a tendency for the parents to abuse drugs of dependence common among adults: alcohol, barbiturates and 'slimming pills'. This, however, does not mean that such antecedents are the cause of drug dependence, they may be just coincidental, or an associated factor.

As for social class, no stratum of society is immune; but as there are more people in the general population who are in skilled, semi-skilled or unskilled occupations, the majority of drug users come from these social groups. As to the peer environment, drug abuse usually starts as a convivial activity on the basis of need or desire to experiment, or to be adventurous, or to be like other friends, or to experience something tabooed or thought to be dangerous by the older members of the community.

Dependence is accidental and luckily affects only a small minority of those who go through the experience of abuse. People who have become dependent and are not 'pushers' (that is, selling drugs to make profit or make a living), rarely induce others to be initiated – at least this is our experience.

But as for identifying the young people who are vulnerable: the simple answer is, we cannot do that for certain. The majority of abusers start in their middle teens, 14 to 17 years of age. The ratio of boys to girls is 5 to 1. Most of the subjects have a history of playing truant regularly, tattooing is common and so is a record of conviction before drug abuse. Their school performance shows a steady decline over the last few years. They usually do not like subjects which require disciplined or logical thinking, for example, science and maths. These are findings based on drug abusers who come to our notice, and do not necessarily imply that those with these attributes will become regular drug abusers. They apply equally to those who become delinquent.

In fact, regular or persistent drug abuse may be just another type of deliquent behaviour, except that it is more damaging to the person in the long run than delinquency. It is better to regard any teenager who is persistently unhappy with his existence, or who finds it very difficult to communicate and relate to conforming peers and adults (with allowances made for the adolescent phase) as vulnerable to regular drug abuse, or, I suppose, to delinquency. Prevention may lie in consistent and compassionate guiding of these people through a prolonged and rather difficult phase of maturing. Most of them do mature out of this difficult and vulnerable phase if supported.

We also need to examine our contradictory attitudes to various drugs. For example, why do we accept with relative complacency, and even condone, drugs like tobacco, alcohol and barbiturates when we know that each one of these drugs is responsible for much human misery and death. Is it because we are used to them, or because their effects are slow and insidious and so escape notice? Or is it because they are abused far more by adults than teenagers?

*Dr Rathod is a consultant psychiatrist working in the Crawley and Horsham areas. His special interest has been the use of narcotic drugs and alcohol, and community care. He has published several papers on these subjects.*

# The extent of the drugs problem

## RICHARD DE ALARCON

Until recently for most people, including many doctors, the mention of drugs of dependence and the people who use them invariably conjured up the picture of a thin, tortured 'junkie' whose whole life is anxiously centred on finding his next supply of heroin. Fortunately in Britain so far this extreme type of drug user is not all that frequent. Many different drugs are being abused and they are being taken in many differing circumstances. As the effects of drug taking depend to some extent on the particular drug or combination of drugs, and the circumstances in which they are usually taken, drug users will vary in severity, in personal appearance and behaviour, and even over whether they are likely or not to stop taking drugs.

This must always be borne in mind if we learn that someone has been taking drugs: there are many types of drugs and many types of drug users. The interviews with adolescent drug-takers in the next section illustrate something of that variety. In any particular case the taking of drugs may be serious, potentially serious, or of relatively little importance. It is not possible to form any opinion about a young person from the simple statement 'he or she has been taking drugs'. And the appropriate response to that situation, by parent or family friend, can only emerge when the situation has been fully explored.

### The growth of the problem – heroin

When in the mid-sixties the increasing abuse of drugs among the young attracted public attention, the news was particularly alarming because the drug concerned was heroin, one of the most potent of the opiates and the one most likely to lead to classical addiction and produce the stereotyped addict. Another alarming feature was the change in the age group and social background of those involved.

Our knowledge at that time was based on information about drug users collected by the Home Office. For many years the Home Office had kept a register of persons dependent on opiates and other drugs listed under the Dangerous Drug Act. However, this register was incomplete, being based mainly on pharmacists' records, Court appearances for illegal possession of drugs, and other official sources. Compulsory notification of heroin and cocaine users to the Home Office did not come into operation until early 1968; before that date doctors could and did prescribe drugs to people who never appeared on the Home Office register. And others using heroin quite illicitly didn't even come to a doctor's attention. A survey I carried out with Dr Rathod in Crawley in 1967 identified 92 heroin users, of whom only eight were known to the Home Office. However incomplete this register may have been before 1968, it still showed quite clearly the changing trends of drug abuse during the sixties. Up to then, there had been a pool of opiate, morphine and heroin users, who developed their dependence as a consequence of treatment with opiates for some painful condition (therapeutic addicts), and a few others (doctors, pharmacists, nurses and so on) who by nature of their work had more opportunities of taking drugs and becoming habituated to them. This group, amounting to between 300 and 400 persons in the whole of the UK, had remained practically constant through the years. Composed mainly of middle-aged, secretive, lone users, it has had therefore small social consequences.

The Home Office figures show that a new group of heroin users began to emerge in the early sixties, increasing in numbers in a dramatic way from 1965 onwards. These were much younger than the 'therapeutic addicts' – only in their late teens or early 20s. In 1959 there were no heroin addicts recorded under the age of 20; by 1966 there were 317. Heroin was the drug of choice rather than morphine; and while the 'therapeutic addicts' belonged mainly to the professional or middle classes, these young drug users showed a more even social distribution, with a large contingent coming from working-class families.

Among this new group, drug taking was not a solitary activity, but an experience that, at least in its initial stages, was shared among peers. It was for many the main topic of conversation, reminiscences of previous experiences were recounted with relish, and heroin was often injected in groups. This social usage, together with the ready availability of the drug, probably played an important role in its rapid spread among young people.

In 1968 and 1969 the figures of heroin users known to the Home Office continued to increase. Notification, however, had become compulsory in early 1968. This meant that the increase could be more apparent than real, for many of the cases reported during this period for the first time had in fact been taking heroin for some years previously. Fortunately the figures for heroin have now stopped rising. Some new cases continue to appear (though many fewer than before) and a number of the previously known heroin users have turned to other drugs. The rising curve of the graph for new cases of heroin abuse has been flattening out since early 1969.

In provincial towns the absence of new cases of heroin abuse in the last year is particularly noticeable. London and other very large towns continue to attract the more serious cases: the anonymity of the metropolis, the greater availability of the drug and the existence of special treatment centres contribute to this attraction.

Setting British opiate abuse in the international scene, the table opposite (from *Drug Addiction*, Office of Health Economics 1967) compares it to countries with a heavy drug problem.

## Other drugs taken by injection – methedrine, physeptone, sleeping tablets

Though the rise of heroin use appears to have been curtailed for the moment, other drugs have to be considered. These drugs vary in popularity according to their availability, their effects and fashion. An interesting example is methedrine, a member of the amphetamine or stimulant group of drugs. In early 1968 injecting this drug became popular among heroin users, who combined it with heroin or took it on its own. Its use soon spread to people who had never used heroin.

This spread caused considerable concern because many regard it as equally if not more dangerous than heroin. Strong psychological dependence develops with its use and while heroin, during the time it is acting in the body, makes the person contented, sleepy and dreamy, methedrine makes him restless, agitated, anxious and aggressive. It can also cause severe mental disturbance.

**Number and rates per million of known narcotic addicts, various selected countries\*, mid 1960s.**

Source: Summary of Annual Reports of Governments relating to opium and other narcotic drugs 1964. UN Commission on narcotic drugs, 1966.

| Country | No. of addicts (approx.) | Rate per million population | Comments |
|---|---|---|---|
| GB (1964) | 750 | 15 | Mainly heroin |
| GB (1966) | 1,300 | 25 | |
| Canada (1965) | 3,600 | 180 | Mainly heroin Includes cannabis |
| Germany (1964) | 4,350 | 80 | Mainly synthetics and morphine Includes amphetamines. |
| Japan (1964) | 9,400 | 100 | Mainly opium, morphine and heroin. |
| Hong Kong (1965) | 10,900 | 2,900 | Mainly heroin |
| Korea (1964) | 15,000 | 540 | Mainly heroin |
| USA (1964) | 55,900 | 290 | Mainly heroin |
| Iran (1965) | 1000,00 – 200,000 (est) | 6,550 | Est. 95 per cent opium, 5 per cent heroin |
| India (1964) | 136,000 opium 200,000 cannabis | 290 420 | |

\*Note: Only those countries which had a substantially higher number of addicts than GB are shown. Many countries reported little or no drug addiction, and for some countries the 1964 UN report showed no figures.

In October 1968 an agreement was reached between the Ministry of Health, the British Medical Association and the main drug manufacturers to reduce production and to supply only hospital pharmacists and not the retail chemists. The effects of this measure were dramatic, and methedrine abuse is now rarely seen.

Restrictions on the use of heroin have led to an increase in the use of physeptone (methadone) – another opiate, though a much weaker one and considered very much 'second best' by the real heroin addict. Again its use has spread in a limited way among experimenters and those who were already taking other drugs. At present it is impossible to assess the extent of its use, as there are no legal limits on prescribing it.

Another practice that has acquired some notoriety in recent months is the injecting of sleeping tablets. These are crushed and then dissolved in water, but as they have not been made specifically for injecting, the solution irritates the tissues at the site of injection, closing up the veins and producing unpleasant ulcers. On account of these side effects, particularly the closing up of available veins for further injections, it is unlikely that this practice will remain popular for long.

**Pep pills**

The amphetamines, a group of stimulant drugs, usually referred to as pep pills, have been a favourite drug of abuse among youngsters for the last six or seven years. Usually taken initially for the experience, 'for kicks', or to keep awake at a dance or party, consumption among those who take to them is quickly increased to up to 60 or 70 pills over a weekend. In provincial towns this heavy weekend consumption is usually associated with all-night parties, migration in groups to other towns, and the frequenting of all-night dance clubs and discotheques and road side cafés.

Those who use amphetamines as their main drug of abuse may associate themselves with certain groups – mods, ex-mods, or skinheads. In some, amphetamine pill taking is restricted to weekends, and they are able to continue at work during the week. In others it will begin to spread to one or more days during the week and take on a more malignant character.

Experimenting with other drugs is, however, common among the amphetamine takers, and a number, as they grow older or the availability of drugs changes in their area, will move to using LSD or injecting. For many, fortunately, it is only another adolescent way of 'living it up' at the weekends, which they grow out of with time. Some years ago it would have been more common to see a group with similar rather 'wild' characteristics drinking heavily.

However, drugs are potentially more dangerous than alcohol. Not only are they illegal and put the person in touch with deviant elements of the population, but dependence and toxic symptoms can appear at a much earlier stage. Therefore, though it is likely that a large number of those who have used them will mature and settle down to a more stable life, there will be some who due to their own personal make-up and a more intensive exposure to the drug scene can fall by the wayside. My own personal impression is that the number who will just try amphetamine a few times and not go on to more serious regular drugtaking is likely to be the majority.

**Sleeping tablets**

Sleeping tablets have been abused by some adults practically from the time they were first used – the dependence usually stemming from prescriptions given initially for medical reasons. But abuse among the young is an event of the last three or four years: poly-drug-users find them one more drug to experiment with. But if readily available and cheap, they will be used more frequently.

**LSD**

Another drug which came on the scene first about three or four years ago is LSD; though it is only during the last two years that it has been used on a large scale. Initially, like cannabis, it was a drug favoured by more intellectual and avant-garde groups: some artists and writers, and some students – mainly the 'drop out' and fringe groups. Also, like cannabis, its use has been associated with 'hippies' and 'flower-children', as an element in the particular way of life of these groups.

Not that a 'hippie-like' appearance automatically involves drug taking. It could simply indicate that the youngster concerned is dressing in the same way and expressing the same ideas as most of the other adolescents in his age group. Enslavement to and stereotyped imitation of peer fashion is a characteristic of teenagers. It is when they are moving among peers who are *regularly* taking drugs that there is reason for concern, as imitation can then extend to drugs.

LSD and other psychedelic drugs are no longer restricted to the groups mentioned above, but their use has extended to youngsters with less intellectual interests. A number of people taking LSD at present were taking amphetamines a few years back. It is too early to say what will be the long-term outcome of this wave of abuse of LSD, particularly among those who take it very frequently and together with large amounts of cannabis.

## Cannabis
Cannabis has not been mentioned up to now because in practice one can say that it is smoked frequently if not regularly by all types of drug users. It is also used in an experimental or limited way by persons who from the clinical point of view are not drug users. For instance, in the typical example of two or three students getting together to experiment with a smoke, the experience may have moral implications for the individual concerned but it will be of no medical or social consequence, except in the case of a very predisposed person. Perhaps it is this type of smoker that is better known to those who advocate a more liberal policy regarding cannabis.

Much more dangerous is the smoking of cannabis within a 'drug-taking' group. Here, drugs are one of the main topics of conversation – if not the only one. Sooner or later the newcomers are likely to try other drugs: the social setting here is of particular importance in the process of escalation from a less dangerous to a more dangerous drug. In fact the social setting is more important than the initial drug itself. The significance of cannabis smoking among the users of other drugs is still in need of study. With this wide range of usage, and users, it is easy to understand why there are no convincing studies in any country on the prevalence of cannabis.

## Poly-drug-users
In this country, only a few dependent drug takers – even those who have taken heroin or methedrine – will restrict themselves to one drug or one group of drugs alone. The majority may have their individual preferences, but will easily move from one drug to another, according to availability. One would like to think that for a young person who has not, perhaps, been injecting a particular drug for long, or using it mainly at weekends, this frequent change from one drug to another wards off severe dependence, and even makes them go off injecting. There are some indications that this may be occurring, but more careful study is required to see if this is the case.

The same experimenting and changing from one drug to another can also be seen among those who take drugs mainly by mouth, even though they may have injected on a few occasions. Pep pills, sleeping tablets, LSD are all part of the drug scene, with cannabis as a common denominator. And cannabis extends to include, usually in a mild way, some who could be considered 'non-drug-taking' elements of society.

Judging from the clinical histories of drug users, a high proportion of them start using drugs while still at school. The drugs first taken may have been pep pills – or as happens more frequently in the last year or two – cannabis or sleeping tablets. With exceptions it seems that this first experience rarely occurs during school hours or on the school premises.

We can summarise the general trends in drug abuse as follows, but it is impossible to report on the situation more specifically:

| | |
|---|---|
| heroin | use stabilised |
| amphetamines | fluctuating (and likely to go down when proposed legislation is passed) |
| barbiturates by injection | recent increase, but decrease likely |
| hypnotics | widespread use among total population and probably rising among the young |
| LSD | rising |
| methedrine | remarkable decrease |
| cannabis | widespread |

As things stand at the moment, it is wise to anticipate that every teenager will be exposed to drugs. As when dealing with other problems which beset this particular age group, parents should not only be aware of the possibility of their occurrence, but also have the foresight to lay, long before any explosion occurs, the foundation for a balanced and solid relationship with the growing child that will survive the break in communication and the various other crises of adolescence, and provide him directly or indirectly with some support.

At the moment it is impossible to predict the ultimate outcome of drug abuse in Britain. There are reasons for a more optimistic view than that held by some authors two or three years ago, but there is no reason for complacency, as many individuals are likely to be affected in the next few years.

**The situation in other countries**
In Japan, where after the Second World War there was a very severe epidemic of amphetamine abuse followed by one of heroin, the Government claim that they have dealt with the problem by intensive police activity aimed at destroying the large drug peddling rings, combined with strong repressive measures against those using drugs, and the provision of extensive treatment facilities. But some of the methods used would not be acceptable in this country.

Sweden, where until recently amphetamine-like substances were the main problem, has only managed partial control so far, though imaginative social preventive measures are being tried out on a small scale in some areas.

In the United States drug abuse has been a problem for many years, particularly in the large cities such as New York and Chicago. However, American social structure and the methods used to deal with the drug problem are so different from ours that few conclusions applicable to the British scene can be drawn.

In Britain restricting supplies can sometimes be effective, as shown in the case of methedrine, but such a measure is not applicable to all types of drugs. LSD for example is at present manufactured illegally and without too much difficulty by competent chemists. It is therefore that much more difficult to control.

The control of the supply and dispensing of a drug of abuse must be applied as early as possible in the spread of its use before a taste, a dependence and therefore a market has been created. However, before supplies of any drug are restricted, careful consideration has to be given as to what drug or activity will take its place and what means will be taken to help those who have already become dependent on that particular drug.

Judging by the course of most past epidemics – be they social or medical – one could predict that the current epidemic of drug abuse will reach a peak and then decline. The question is, how much immediate suffering will it entail and what will be the long term consequences for those who have succumbed during it? Secondly, will we be left after the acute phase of the epidemic is over with a higher rate of drug abuse in the general population than there was before the outbreak started? The answers to these two questions are impossible to predict.

*Dr de Alarcon was born in San Francisco in California of Spanish parents. He started his medical studies in Central America, qualified in Spain and subsequently re-qualified in England. He was registrar at the Maudsley Hospital, London for four years and then worked as a consultant psychiatrist at the London University Institute of Education. He has been on the psychiatric staff of the Medical Research Council Clinical Psychiatry Unit at Graylingwell Hospital, Chichester, since December 1968. When he was consultant psychiatrist to the Horsham and Crawley Psychiatric Services he saw the first cases of heroin abuse that came to light in that area. This provided the field for epidemiological studies into the prevalence and mode of spread of heroin abuse in the area. Dr de Alarcon is at present undertaking a more extensive project on the same subject that will embrace several towns under the auspices of the MRC.*

# Talking to young drug takers

## SASHA MOORSOM

It is almost inevitable that every young person will come in contact with drugs, in some form or another, sometime between the ages of 13 and 18. They may try out some of their parents' pep pills or sleeping pills; they may be offered a smoke at a party. How they react to this initial encounter, and whether drugs become a force that dominates their lives depends on so many things – the company they keep, their relationships at home, even, sometimes, how much pocket money they get. Drugs are part of the background of their culture and they are quite likely to know rather more about them, and certainly to have experienced more of their effects, than their parents. The following interviews illustrate some of the ways in which young people approach drugs, the different effects they have, and the very different situations created for the parents concerned.

### Peter

Peter was sitting in the New Horizon Youth Centre in Soho – a day centre for addicts and others who have nowhere else to go. Outside it was pouring with rain. He was wearing a torn yellow football vest – a relic of his schooldays. The knuckles of his fingers were raw, the right hand bound up with a bandage. (He had made a tourniquet on his right arm before injecting himself. The drug had worked so fast that he'd fallen asleep before he had time to get the tourniquet off, an accident that could have been fatal to his hand.) His face, though drawn, was gentle and intelligent. He had that morning been chucked out finally, he said, by his parents. He still had the grey vestiges of a black eye his father had given him the week before. He didn't blame his father, he said. He just got so angry he couldn't control himself. As for his mother – he made a gesture of someone mowing people down with a machine gun – that's what she thought should happen to all addicts.

Peter is the fourth of five children of Irish parents. His mother and father had very little education but he and his brothers and sisters passed the 11-plus. As a Roman Catholic he was sent out of his own district to a Catholic grammar school.

We were regarded as slum brats by some of the masters. I hated it from the word go. I was always in trouble, getting the cane.

He played truant frequently.

It was a very constructive truancy. I had a baker's round and a butcher's round. I gave most of the bread (money) to my mother. She didn't ask too many questions because she liked the money.

His truancies got bolder and bolder, covered up by forged notes – 'I used to hire out my services to the other boys' – until for a six-week stretch he never went to school at all. Finally they caught up with him and at 14 he was expelled.

38

In the masters' eyes I wasn't worth anything academically. I didn't like them so I didn't want to do anything for them.

He had never wanted to go to the grammar school at all:

The secondary modern was the envy of all the boys around. A lot of my pals had managed to get expelled and get back to the secondary modern.

But the local authority decided he should go to another grammar school – a good decision as it turned out.

I was knocked out with it. I never played truant. I took a few mornings off to go to the snooker hall but that was just growing up. I got in the A stream in maths. I was knocked out by English. Art was great, we had a really hip art teacher. And there were these girls which was just great after the monastic life.

In spite of all this he still decided to leave as soon as he was 15, because he wanted money.

I asked if I could leave. The head sent for my mother and said 'Look, this boy's work is very good. It'll be an awful waste if he leaves'. I wasn't persuaded. I left just after the Christmas term.

His first job in a big electrical firm lasted three months. He started taking pep pills – purple hearts – in cafés in the West End. After that he flitted from job to job.

My record was a quarter of an hour in one job. I was five minutes late so I got paid for ten minutes' work.

At 17 he was stopped for driving without a licence.

I was fixing my brother-in-law's scooter. In order to fix it I had to try it. I was caught.

Then he did a spell in Borstal for being a passenger on the back of a stolen scooter. 'The screws were animals, I hated them'. Three months after he was let out on licence he had gravitated to hard drugs – methedrine and heroin. If the police hadn't picked him up and taken him back to prison he would, according to the prison medical officer, have soon been dead.

When he left Borstal, he went to live with a family who had befriended him. He became deeply attached to the wife – 'We had good vibes' – and began to have an affair with her, but:

I felt myself becoming so much obsessed with her that I thought, Christ, I'd better start scoring.

He found himself cited in a divorce case. In his view this predicament drove him back to drugs. The drugs estranged him from the one relationship he cared about. He is now a registered addict.

She says she doesn't know if she can stand it any more. But I will not seek an alternative if my affaire is finished. They think, the people here, that my trouble started because I lost my religion. I had a strict Catholic upbringing. But by the time I was 16 I'd stopped going to Church. I seem to be beset by calamities. I think it's Divine Providence, my punishment.

Peter is 22.

## Marie

Marie is a pretty 18-year-old from France, rather shy and reserved, who has just taken her Baccalaureat. Her father left home when she was seven. She first experimented a few months ago.

*Marie*: My mother had gone away for three days. A friend of mine brought some ether round to our flat. He wanted to sniff it at home but he couldn't because his mother was there and it smells too strong. I didn't want to do it. He began sniffing and got turned on and started talking about Baudelaire. I think I was a bit curious so I took some too.

*Q*: What effect did it have?

*Marie*: It was as if I was dreaming, but at the same time I knew what I was doing. I remember closing the top of the bottle very carefully. I kept thinking I was going to wake up. I got more and more silent. Everything was going on inside my head. It lasted about two or three hours and I liked it because it was so strange. Afterwards I felt ill. The smell hung around the flat and it was horrible. I burnt joss sticks in my room to get rid of it and the mixture was awful. My mother came back the next day and said: 'What a terrible smell!'

*Q*: Did you try it again?

*Marie*: Yes, a month later with another friend. I found a bottle of ether in my mother's cupboard and I asked him to try it with me. His eyes were staring out of his head. We played pop and it was a new experience of music for me. My mother came home in the middle. I was completely gone. I couldn't care less. I think I was a bit rude to her, I told her to get out. I'd been painting and my friend said we'd used some ether to clean up some split paint. Luckily she believed him. Afterwards I filled the bottle up with water and put it back in her cupboard. While I was high I painted a face. It was really frightening. The eyes were extraordinary – round and staring.

*Q*: What else have you tried?

*Marie*: Hash. A friend took me to someone's house and there were about eight people there. They were passing round two pipes. There were some beautiful vases on a shelf – I noticed them as soon as I came into the room. At one moment I had the most strange experience. I could see these marvellous shapes and colours – the vases – through my friend's body. But they were the other side of him – it was extraordinary. Three of us lay on the bed and passed the pipe around. My friend started laughing and laughing. Then we started laughing. We couldn't stop. We were all laughing so much we were crying. Afterwards we felt drowsy, but when I went home I couldn't sleep. Next day I was very tired but I had to go to school. My friend had stomach trouble for two weeks after.

*Q*: Have you ever spent money on drugs?

*Marie*: I've never bought anything myself. I wouldn't know how to get it or whether it was mixed with something else. I take it if I'm offered it with friends. They've made such a campaign against drugs in France that it makes you interested. There's something on television about it every day. It pushes you towards it.

## Nina, Simon, Jim, Rachel

*At a week-end pop concert there was a huge crowd of young people from about 14 to 22 queuing up for tickets: girls in long satin dresses or Indian cotton, one with an ancient fox fur round her neck. 'Meet Basil Brush', she said gaily as she joined her friend. There were crushed velvet jeans, tie-dyed vests, fringed suede jackets, one or two bovver-boots boys. I talked to several 14 and 15 year olds and tape recorded the conversations.*

40

## Nina

Nina, 14, had long fair hair like a curtain either side of her face. She lives with her mother and step-father and goes to an academic girl's school. She smoked her first hash six months ago.

*Nina*: It just made me feel further off the ground than usual. I didn't think it was particularly exciting. It lasted half-an-hour or an hour. Then I did it quite a lot with anybody I could find, with people from school or people I met out of school, about once or twice a week.

*Q*: Did you get to like it more?

*Nina*: Not really. That's why I stopped. It was getting boring.

*Q*: Why did you want to do it then?

*Nina*: Oh, to find out about it. You know, everybody was going on about how great it was. But it didn't give me anything I couldn't get, you know, just being around.

*Q*: Where did you get the hash from?

*Nina*: Oh, friends, and friends of friends. It's all a sort of network of friends. You used to be able to get it from school before they started tightening down on things. They found some behind a tree. What it was doing there I've no idea.

*Q*: Was it important to you at the time?

*Nina*: Yeah, you know, I'm glad I tried it. Now I know what it's like I don't really want to do it any more. I've found out you can get good things out of life without it. I might try something else when I'm older but I don't really feel the need now.

*Q*: Did your parents know you'd smoked?

*Nina*: One of my friend's parents found out about my friend smoking and they told my parents and my parents asked me. They didn't look too angry when they asked me so I risked it. Now they know I'm glad. They didn't really mind. I mean they've tried it. It doesn't do anything in particular to you. It doesn't make you wildly irresponsible or anything.

*Q*: Do you think you have a good relationship with your parents?

*Nina*: Er . . . yes. They let me do practically anything except stay out all night, which is reasonable. I used to argue with them a lot about whether I should be allowed out later but we've come to an agreement now. If I tell them where I'm going, tell them what time I'll be back, they say 'Don't be home that late.' So then we sort of compromise.

## Simon

Simon and Jim were laughing, lively 15-year-olds from an old-fashioned boys' grammar school. Simon's parents were separated.

*Q*: Does it matter to you that hash is against the law?

*Simon*: No. Actually I think that because it's against the law it's much more fun. To know that it's in the bottom of your pocket when you pass a police car is much more fun than if you can go and buy it like two ounces of Typhoo. It's nice to know that you're doing something illegal, I think.

41

*Q*: Do your parents know you smoke?

*Simon*: My mum doesn't even know I smoke cigarettes. She'd hit the roof. I don't get on very well with her. I just walked out of the house this morning because she wouldn't let me come here. It's very binding. I can't do anything really.

*Q*: Do you think you know more about drugs than her?

*Simon*: Yeah. Because she reads in the straight press like *The Times* about drug and sex orgies in Hyde Park and things like that – the deadly weed and so on. But it's not like that. You can never really know what it's like unless you've experienced it. The first time I tried it was at the school camp. Jim asked me if I'd like some and we went into the woods and had a smoke behind the trees. It was just getting dark and after that we went back into the tent and went to bed. The master was flashing his torch around but he didn't notice anything.

*Q*: Would you take any other drug?

*Simon*: If it was a fix I wouldn't have it. I'd take speed (methedrine) or acid (LSD). If I wasn't paying for it, even if I didn't know him, I'd have it.

*Jim*: I take acid. I've had two bad trips. They were bad but not bad enough to put me off.

*Simon*: They put me off (*laughter*).

**Jim**

*Q*: How much do you use drugs?

*Jim*: I smoke about five times a day. When I'm at school I make up for it in the evenings. I wouldn't take H or cocaine. It's not very nice stuff. I don't like the buzz.

*Q*: How much pocket money do you get a week?

*Jim*: About £2 10s.

*Q*: How much of that do you spend on drugs?

*Jim*: £2 10s (*laughter*). I buy records occasionally too.

*Q*: Do your parents know anything about it?

*Jim*: My dad knows I've been speeding. I came home and my pupils were very large and that, and I was out of my brain. He sort of cottoned on to it because he knows quite a lot about drugs. He told me not to take speed any more because it's very bad for you. So I said OK and I gave it up. My dad knows a lot more about drugs than I do.

*Q*: What was your bad trip like?

*Jim*: You see lots of horrors like rats and dogs and eyes. Everything sort of goes grey, and you feel very scared. You feel uneasy wherever you are. But it didn't last very long, it wasn't a very bad trip. It didn't put me off at all.

*Q*: Do you think you'll go on taking things all your life?

*Jim*: I shouldn't think so, no. Once you've experienced it quite often you sort of get used to its effect. It becomes a drag like everyday life. So you have a dose of normality and get a buzz from that.

*Q*: Do you smoke at home?

*Jim*: If I do it at home I do it with my sister. My parents don't notice because we burn joss sticks.

*Q*: Do you think you should be able to talk about it to them openly?

*Jim*: Yes, because smoking cannabis is not very bad.

*Simon*: That's my ambition – to share it with my mother (*laughter*).

### Rachel
Rachel aged 15, plump and a little dozy, talked about her first experience of drugs:

*Rachel*: The first thing, I think, was dubes (pills). I took things like Mandrax and Black Bombers and hash. Last of all I've taken acid and speed.

*Q*: How old were you when you started?

*Rachel*: I must have been 13, nearly 14. I had some friends who were taking it, friends from school, and they offered it to me. I quite liked Mandrax then. They're sleepers. You swallow them. The overdose is six and then you die. I felt out of the world, not altogether there. Your mind's completely spaced. You are not with anything physically around you, and then you touch something and your whole body tingles. They've been put on the danger list now and I think that's a good thing. People freak out on them. They take too many. Black Bombers are to keep you awake. But I didn't particularly like them because they keep you awake all night. I still smoke hash but I don't take Black Bombers any more.

*Q*: Would you take heroin?

*Rachel*: No, because I think it's a very bad drug. It's worse than anything. You can get hooked on heroin much better than you can get hooked on acid. You have to trip quite a lot to get hooked on acid. I had a friend who freaked out on heroin and he was so bad it just put me off for life. They said 'Have you eaten today?' and he said 'Yes, a piece of chocolate cake.' That's all he'd eaten that day and it was late evening. He was really ill.

*Q*: Do you think you could get hooked on drugs?

*Rachel*: Well, anybody could become dependent on drugs if they're not careful enough. I use them quite a lot but it's not as much as some people. I have them about once, twice, maybe three times a week but not much more than that. We smoke about three times a week on average, take acid about every three weeks or so.

*Q*: What's your father's job?

*Rachel*: He's a medical representative for a big drug firm. He's given me drugs and he's shown me drugs that he was going to sell on the side.

*Q*: What has he given you?

*Rachel*: Hash, Black Bombers and Mandrax. But I think he mainly gives me them because he doesn't want me to take things like acid.

*Q*: How did he find out?

*Rachel*: Once I was smoking with my friend and my father came up and saw the cigarette case with hash in it. He told my mother and he said that he'd throw it away. But in fact he didn't. He kept it and smoked it himself. Then my mother found it so he really had to throw it away. My mother hasn't the slightest idea what she's talking about. She knows cannabis is cannabis and that's about it. She just doesn't know the first thing about it. She's worried that I know so much.

*Q*: Has she ever tried anything herself?

*Rachel*: You're joking!

*Q*: Why are you on probation?

*Rachel*: I got busted. I've been put on two years' probation and a year's medical care. I stayed out at night without my parents' consent or anything. I stayed round at a friend's flat and we were having a smoke there and the police came in and took us back to the station and said: 'You've been reported missing and why didn't you go home and you're only 15' and all that. They found five lbs worth of grass and 120 acid tablets in the flat. Now I have to go and see a psychiatrist once every two weeks. It's not doing me any good. I suppose they want to see if there's anything wrong with me mentally.

### Sarah

*A 17-year-old girl, on the run from approved school, wrote this about herself in the New Horizon Youth Centre*:

I left boarding school to go and live with my parents. Even though I was only 11 at the time friction started to build up in the family mainly over me. It was when I'd been home just over a year that I started to mix in with the geezers around Upminster. Consequently I began downing blues after a month.

I met a guy who lived near me. He went up West so I started to go with him. He was fixing meth but turned me on to H. I kept getting worse and worse and when I was 15 I got busted for shit (heroin). When it was reported in court that I was hooked on H they committed me to a mental hospital for three months.

I went through a hell of a rough time in there. Everything I ate in the first five days I brought up, but worst of all was the stomach cramp. I hate pain and was almost ready to kill myself but when the doctor saw what a state I was getting into he stepped up the pills I was getting and consequently I was too dozy to do much. After a month I was feeling fine, so I absconded but came back after a week as I seemed to be on a continuous come-down. After another two weeks I was allowed home.

I behaved myself for about a month, kept clean and started courting a straight guy who had more or less refused to walk on the same side of the street as me a couple of months before.

Then one day I bunked off school and went up to Hampstead to see Jerry. I got so stoned I almost flaked out. He phoned up home and told my mother I was staying there for the night as I was too upset to go home. He told her I wanted to fix again and he'd stopped me – the bloody liar. He gave me three grains of H and a works to take back with me the following morning. Natch, I soon got hooked again and my dad threatened to stop my allowance. I was getting £8 a week then – we're very well off.

It didn't matter 'cause in July I got busted again, this time for H. I don't know how, but I got off with another three months in hospital and two years' supervision. This time they put me out for five days, waking me up three times a day. It was much better than my first cure.

44

But when I came round I found out that one of my old mates was on lease from approved school there, and I bunked off again with him. We hitched round the coast from Torquay to Newquay. In the end I gave the pair of us up, as neither of us was strong enough to doss out. I had to go on remand and back to court. They let me off with just the same supervision, thanks to my head-shrinker who said that he thought being inside would break me altogether.

I started going up to Hampstead again and a few months later I got busted by the Drug Squad for 2lb weight and I was back on remand. I got committed just after my 16th birthday and this time it was up to three years' approved school, fucking bastards.

For a while everything went fine. Then leave unsettled me and I decided to abscond with a friend. We made for the Dilly as it's quite an easy place even though it's choked with fuzz. We picked up two buskers and dossed the first night with them.

On Tuesday night I met Harry in here. He turned me on to H again but, man, it's my last fix. Soon we are hoping to go up to Glasgow. Hope we make it without getting busted.

I'm just wondering how my life'll turn out now. I guess I won't be satisfied till everything's OK. If I go back to approved school I'll probably get transferred to Borstal or a locked approved school. If I don't I'll just bunk it again.

*Sasha Moorsom, a former editor of WHERE, is now working as a free-lance journalist and teaching part-time in a London primary school.*

# The crisis of adolescents

## ANDREW CROWCROFT

I chose this rather ungrammatical title because it continues to be my experience that many parents expect a child to become an adult without difficulty. Many years ago Margaret Mead showed how growing up in Samoa went smoothly and remarkably unremarkably. But it has long since been agreed that in Western cultures adolescence normally is abnormal. It produces all kinds of new problems and anxieties, commonly acutely. Indeed, in our culture we should worry about the boy or girl who too easily, without a tear, gives up childhood for that no-man's land, adolescence, a no-man's land exploited more by manufacturers than catered for by a sentimental society, which believes it cares for the young.

### School experience

School is compulsory. It can be therefore, as an institution, the scapegoat for a wide variety of hostile feelings, the true original target being obscured. Early adolescence is a very powerful age for the formation of tight groups, of gangs of boys and girls. One of the psychological functions of such a gang, an element that keeps a natural group (as apart from the synthetic therapeutic group) together, is dislike of another group or individual. Here again, one finds paradox. Adolescence has been called a 'crisis of identity', when all the basic questions of life are asked. Where do I come from, who am I, where am I going, what does life mean? All these questions still emerge, modified only by the literacy, intelligence and background of the adolescent. Yet such individuation, such a Renaissance-man feeling for existence, leads into a group, rather than into a solitary intellectual journey.

So the odd-adolescent-out is the solitary one, and he must be judged on his merits. It might be a signal of emotional trouble when a school report says a child is solitary. A few children and adolescents are truly solitaries and just do not need others much (highly-gifted children, often earlier terribly lonely, first come to social flowering now). Adolescence, in school or out, is a time of stubbornness, moodiness and mood changes. Aggression is often shown by unwillingness, a surly manner, sulking. It is an inconsistent time emotionally. In general, then, the loner in adolescence, particularly if his introversion has deepened and if his mood remains rather fixed and sad, is in need of more help than perhaps even very understanding parents can give.

The adolescent who joins a gang may be normal enough in his gregarious drive. The group itself, however, may be sick, a body of young people compulsively reaching for what they think to be valuable, merely because it is what we oldies condemn. A group philosophy can be diseased.

We have said that school can be the recipient of many of the hostile feelings of that age group. 'They', 'them', 'authority', any of the social structures that can be seen unconsciously as critical parental figures, invite attack. This can inform the adolescent's mood. Therefore we can understand how the adolescent pushes against them. He, or she, indeed, seems to hunger for causes, for something to thrust against. A point of departure. A way of saying, 'I am I, I am not you, here and terribly now. I cannot wait. I only find myself by not being you'. As with a toddler, who finds himself first, in a way, when he can totter away on his own feet from his possessing mother. Stress is *wanted*, a difference. The generation gap is made of growth, a welcoming of stress, search, struggle, separation.

But how much stress? Some schools demand incredible levels of conformity, and assert all their authority in gaining – or attempting to gain – it. Such schools expect to regulate how a teenager dresses, the length of his hair, what he does out of school. Loyalty is demanded, and an acceptance of the existing class and social structure. In return, particularly in the more academic schools, are dangled all the academic treasures: entry to the sixth form, the begrudging words of praise. These kinds of schools take more than school subjects as their brief. The personality is also to be moulded – 'character' as they say. Where this approach relates somehow to the nature of the biological stage: giving adventure, outlets or initiative, opinion, responsibility – fine. Where the school is infected with school-marmitis, petty tyranny, over-control, the young can begin to fade out academically. The whole scene has become irrelevant, for them, to life. I have seen adolescents with an IQ of over 140 (*ie* in the top $\frac{1}{2}$ per cent of the population for intelligence) fail in schools like this. Apart from bad school reports, the adolescent from such schools at home seems 'fed up' all the time, argumentative, bloody minded, and/or a 'big baby'. The drop out, however, is not a dullard. Many are among our brightest, as I have said.

It is in the early teens that learning difficulties become more crucial. With our overcrowded classes, many children reach secondary school barely literate. In secondary school, many of the types of help – remedial classes and so on – of primary school days are less commonly available. In any case, it is only rarely that plain coaching will really help now, if the child has come from a reasonable, if crowded, primary school. It is late, but not too late for psychological intervention. Many cases of learning problems are embedded in family problems, and are merely expressed by the 'low achiever'. Girls seem more often missed by the pundits than boys, because we continue to have higher expectations of boys than girls, and therefore take boys' education more seriously. If an adolescent seems to be finding his work too much for him, it is worth talking to his teacher. On the one hand, the young man or woman may be hung up on learning; on the other, the parents may be too ambitious for him or her, unrealistic, too pushing. The child in either case may be responding by an apparent 'laziness', or a maddening refusal to take the situation seriously. If pushed too hard, he may alternatively begin to truant, turn to delinquency and anti-social acts, determined to express himself somehow, or to 'deserve' the criticism he has felt unfair. An adolescent of different temperament (and history) may become withdrawn. A girl will more usually become over-passive when under stress. There is a highly felt 'them' (the oldies) versus 'us'. If we neatly collude by ill-judged coercion, the more flamboyant will turn to more anti-social responses still.

## Pressure to qualify

Success has rightly been called the 'bitch goddess'. It is nice if the adolescent feels a reasonable inner determination to succeed. Are parents always sure that their own parental wishes for the success of their offspring come from pure concern for the future of the young? Psychiatrists still discover, in exploring the feelings of parents, that parental disappointments in their children spring from

47

the parents' own earlier failures, that they wish their children to do what they failed to do themselves. Of course parents wish better for their children. But this must never mean at the price of an adolescent's happiness, or be a target beyond his intellectual means. Humans need *some* anxiety in order to learn. Too much is as destructive as could-not-care-less.

Here we must also mention how imbecile are so many schools about tests and exams. Success and failure are made as black and white as the race war. Despite all the scientific, experimental work on the unreliability of examinations, the results of mock GCEs can determine which real GCEs can be taken. This can obviously affect a whole life, in that universities ask for particular O levels and A levels. Many sixth forms have an unconscious 'hierarchy' of pupils – those destined for Oxbridge, for other universities, for polytechnics, teacher training colleges or other further education colleges, like a dying sigh! Schools having sixth forms like these seem to be having a disease we can call 'Oxbridge – or bust'. Here Oxbridge means win. Elsewhere means fail. Yet what are the educational *facts*? What does the individual adolescent need? Which is the best college for *him*? Oxbridge in fact – let us leave snobs out of it – does not do everything as well as other people. None of the social sciences, for example, I would think, are well done there. There is lots of scope for theology, but few care! Parents should find out which university or college in the UK does best what is best for their child.

For all the difficulty sometimes of getting near to an adolescent, realistic encouragement is a better bet than bullying. It is an attitude that can help the adolescent be a success, and also help him over academic failure. In life, we can learn at any age, quite often more from failure than success: how life goes on afterwards; that people still like us, for ourselves; that it is not the end of the world. To fail is better than to 'drop out'.

**Career choices**
We know that, while intelligence, as ordinarily defined, stops growing at about 16, physical growth continues much longer, and experience can be gained throughout life. In the desire to be independent, a teenager can be too precipitate in 'defining' himself, in committing himself to a career. He may give us an indication that he wants to break away from us – for we have been altogether too much for him – by aiming too high or too low for a career. If we have not let him decide much for himself before, as an over-compensation for this he may cling passionately to the most unlikely choice of career. If we do battle, the outcome will be like a toilet training battle. Both sides will lose. A girl, insecure as a separate person, can be overcome and go from her family straight into a teenage liaison or marriage, with no freedom between childhood and this pseudo-grown-up, essentially dependent, relationship. The possibility of trial-and-error learning, of recognition that emotional growth based on the adolescent's experience of life is possible, is needed on both sides – parents and teenager. Where the teenager is totally, stubbornly lost in dreams of success, in terms of career, entirely unrealistically, he or she is at risk to make the dreams last longer with the help of drugs.

The term 'academic' is frequently a pejorative term. So frequently, and especially in the more academic schools, children of 13, 14 or 15 are expected to know what they want to do in life, and, as a measure, decide which GCEs they will take. Lucky the boy or girl who knows! On the one hand academic schools tend to be infantilising, coercive, controlling. On the other, they expect a child to be 'free' to choose. Lucky, in such a mischance, the child who has a parent who gives the teenager time to choose – and tells the headmaster so. There is a very real group of adolescents who were forced to make premature choices, and half way through the GCE rat race begin to fade, as their false convictions become obvious to them themselves. The failure may manifest itself later, at university, with the very intelligent.

## Sex and life style

It does not help to say 'when I was your age. . .' if only because this bores the young, and they are older than we were at their age, anyway, because physical adolescence is speeding up. Girls start having periods three months earlier every 10 years. Our culture cannot have produced Havelock Ellis, Marie Stopes, Norman Hare 50 years ago, and a thousand imitations since, and remain surprised that virginity is now often a joke among the young. Yet of all things causing the increasing 'generation gap', this seems the most powerful. In these contraceptive days, many young people have a lot of sex. Yet the reliable scientific studies do not show they are promiscuous. In many ways they are more honourable than their parents, and go to bed with one another because they like one another, without any blackmail about marriage and all that.

Sexual activity of the adolescent still alarms many parents, while the contemporary adolescent is calm about it. Like computers and electronics, he and she often take sex for granted, while their parents, often more neurotic in this respect, fumble, worry and fail in it. Parents are enormously envious of the young in this respect. Freud helped them and not us.

It is only when the child becomes an adolescent that an idea of romantic love becomes possible. Before that sex interests children, but it is not much more than what bunny rabbits or mice do too. Romantic love means this is what one's parents do, and what a teenager does – within a relationship. He or she who doubts their capacity for this – emotionally or physically – may seek escape from the responsibility of sex through drugs. Many a teenager who feared to fail sexually, or who felt he had failed (not knowing practice makes perfect) turned to another, 'chemical' maturity – pep pills, or cannabis, or whatever, where erection or orgasm was irrelevant.

## Parental conflict

People who come from broken homes often end up breaking up their own marriages. Divorce is almost 'inherited'. This illustrates how the child identifies with his parents. He takes as a model the kind of person his father was, and has expectations of his wife which often correspond with how his mother seemed to him. All this happens by example, whether parents like it or not. It is really no good saying 'don't do as I do, do as I say'. Yet a teenager is a frightful moralist. Where it seems to him there is a lie being lived out by his parents, an hypocrisy, a deadness, he will want to reject this. If he is healthy enough, his 'adolescent rebellion' may be sublimated into politics and causes. If he is unable healthily to turn necessity into a virtue, he may try to smother reality by drugs, a chemical aid to daydreams, where there are no problems, while the dream lasts.

Over all the various areas we have so briefly touched on, there can be conflict between a teenager and his parents. Too much, or too little interest in his schooling; too much concern, or indifference to success or failure in exams and qualifications; unreal views as to his career; fatuous, Victorian notions of sexual morality (particularly repellant where all else is materialistic and provincial).

## Values

I hope it has not been too obvious how difficult it is to write both briefly and in generalisations about the adolescent. Each statement can be contradicted by a particular experience. Yet for those of us who concern ourselves with the teenager, the main impression is impressive. Their liveliness and curiosity and that healthy rebellion against authority, injustice and the wrongs in society remain. Our problem with drugs does not concern the majority. It concerns the 'orally fixated', the over-reacting dependent and immature (who thus get dependent on substances and pushers), the depressed. It is not a matter of mere stupidity. Many brilliant students – who cannot tolerate loneliness, who have an over-developed idea of the futility of life (like some hero of a 19th-century Russian novel) are victims. Despite minds which could easily work out the death sentence hard drugs imply, they succumb.

Somewhere we must mention values. The values of our society. We are materialistic, and largely non-religious, We tend all to feel politically impotent. If it does not seem to matter what we do, why not 'drop out', via drugs? Drug taking has joined 'crime' as a function of an industrial society. Crime has been called 'the folk-art of the poor'. Drugs seem to be more inhuman. They have programmed the dreaming of the otherwise distressed. Levi-Strauss called dreams one of the machines (with music and myth) for the suppression of time. Drug dreams suppress life in the end.

## Conclusions

We have been concerned with the vulnerability of a particular age group. What do we look for? Which features of adolescence should make us seek help for them?

1 – regression – any *massive* return to childish behaviour;

2 – rigidity – too great demands on himself, obsessionality, perfectionism;

3 – inability to generalise his family relationships into general, social ones;

4 – appropriateness of mood – is he, or she, too sad or elated considering the circumstances?

5 – how reasonably 'in the world' is the youngster? Does his or her mind seem in the world as we know it?

6 – does the teenager dread the future?

7 – is our adolescent persistently (as apart from transiently) phobic for school, a truanter, *persistently* stealing (we have all stolen something) lying, withdrawn, alone?

Let us realise the world has changed. We, the adults, are already corrupted by a world that has already died. We may fatally moralise too long about the adolescent when, by their behaviour, they are simply crying, 'help me'.

*Dr Andrew Crowcroft is consultant psychiatrist to the Queen Elizabeth Hospital for Children, the John Scott Health Centre, the Harbrough School for Autistic Children. He is also a member of the academic board at the London University Institute of Child Health.*

# Rescue services for adolescents

## JOHN PAYNE

For many years now psychologists have classified adolescence as a period of transition, a complex and awkward link between childhood and adulthood. It is a transition that does not take place overnight and is not so much a step as an incline, an incline which is getting steeper as children are maturing more and more rapidly.

Idealism or 'high-mindedness' is an essential element of adolescence. There is a need for someone or something outside of the adolescent to fulfil and complete himself. This quest of self-evaluation and searching for some workable relationship with society as a whole can take the form of an interest in religion, philosophy, politics, morality and social justice in the widest sense. One form of idealism is a search for a perfect world and perfect people. In some cases, if the real world is seen to be unhappy and unsatisfactory, then an exaggeratedly happy world must be created out of fantasy and imagination. For some young people imagination and fantasy need more stimulation than can be achieved by a flexing of intellectual muscles, and they experiment with short term artificial aids – drugs. The bleaker the inner life of the adolescents concerned, the more important drugs are likely to become.

Almost without exception dependence on drugs is indicative of emotional disturbance and uncertainty. In some cases it represents serious psychiatric disturbance. When a family is faced with this kind of trouble, what help can parents call on?

### The help available: 'extremely patchy'

The sad fact is that facilities, both statutory and voluntary, for helping adolescents with mild or severe psychiatric problems are extremely patchy. Almost without exception adolescents with psychiatric symptoms need special hospital provision. Accordingly the Ministry of Health laid down guidelines in 1964 indicating the number of special adolescent units each regional hospital board should provide. The recommendation was for a *minimum* provision of 20 to 25 places per million population. The 1964 situation was that seven out of the 15 regional hospital boards already had such units in operation but they provided only 180 beds across England and Wales. It was hoped that provision would be stepped up rapidly. It was not. By 1969, five years after the Ministry of Health guidelines were established, the number of beds was still well below the advised levels.

The table on the next page gives the provision of psychiatric beds in special adolescent units by the 15 regional hospital boards, compared with Ministry of Health's minimum specification. The boards are listed in order of their failure to create the necessary facilities.

51

| Hospital board | beds required | beds provided | per cent provision |
|---|---|---|---|
| Manchester | 91 –114 | 0 | 0 |
| North-east Metropolitan | 68 – 85 | 0 | 0 |
| South Western | 62 – 77 | 0 | 0 |
| Welsh | 54 – 68 | 0 | 0 |
| Oxford | 38 – 47 | 0 | 0 |
| Newcastle | 62 – 77 | 6 | 9 |
| East Anglia | 34 – 43 | 10 | 26 |
| South-east Metropolitan | 71 – 88 | 23 | 29 |
| North-west Metropolitan | 84 – 105 | 30 | 32 |
| Sheffield | 92 – 115 | 35 | 34 |
| Liverpool | 45 – 56 | 18 | 36 |
| Birmingham | 102 – 127 | 42 | 37 |
| Leeds | 64 – 79 | 44 | 62 |
| South-west Metropolitan | 65 – 81 | 48 | 66 |
| Wessex | 39 – 49 | 30 | 68 |

Thus five boards have made absolutely no provision at all, and not one of the 15 reaches even the minimum level for facilities. Only three, in fact, are over half way towards an acceptable situation.

The chronic scarcity of facilities means that many highly disturbed adolescents are denied the proper form of care, to the despair of their families and the professional mental health workers who try to help them.

The near impossibility of securing a special unit bed for a patient is likely to affect, too, a psychiatrist's recommendation concerning the treatment of a disturbed adolescent. Many admit readily that they have stopped recommending placement in such units because it is a waste of time to go through the motions when the effort is bound to come to nothing. So instead they settle for 'second-best'. And the second-best that is available is approved school.

### An unattractive option
The general mental illness hospitals are an unattractive option. For since special units and wards for mentally ill children are rare, and those for adolescents are, as we have seen, pitifully underprovided, the outcome for about seven thousand young people a year is a bed in an adult ward in a psychiatric hospital. Many who are admitted as informal patients are not slow to discharge themselves after brief experience of that situation.

So, often, approved school seems a better choice. It has been estimated that a third of the children and adolescents in approved schools are there for that reason. They are in need of sustained psychiatric treatment to correct serious maladjustment or mental illness. And it is their tragedy that such treatment is beyond the scope of approved schools, which were never intended to fulfil such a major psychiatric function.

Adolescents who become sufficiently disturbed to need hospitalisation, or whose 'acting out' goes beyond the limits of the law, represent the 'severe' section of the wide spectrum of adolescent psychiatric disturbance. The situation for those young people and their families is extremely bleak. None the less, there is a much wider problem of less severely disturbed adolescents whose problems do not come to light because of brushes with the Courts and the hospitals.

Often these problems are too mild to be picked up by the statutory social services: intervention by the state is not imperative. But their need of help is extremely urgent. What facilities can they, and their families, turn to to sort out the trouble?

## Undergraduates: a privileged minority

Just one group is privileged – university and college students: not only do appropriate facilities exist for them, but they will be in contact with people who have enough perception to direct them towards using those facilities.

The network of Student Health Services, based on the universities, provide the most comprehensive preventative and treatment facilities for the psychiatric disturbances of late adolescence – and it is a desperately needed service. In fact practically all the universities have them, and they are well used. Dr Nicholas Malleson, of London University's Research Unit for Student Problems, records that 13 per cent of the total student population at University College, London, were treated in a single year for severe (2·6 per cent) or minor (10 per cent) psychiatric disorders. Figures for Leeds and Sussex are much the same.

Similarly a special committee of the Royal College of Physicians concerned with the student health service has collected evidence which shows that five students in a thousand miss half a term or more each year because of illness, and of these, two are psychiatric and three are medical or surgical in nature. So of illnesses which seriously disrupt a university student's education, about 40 per cent are psychiatric.

A university is a specialised community, with a particular pattern of selection, varying techniques for processing its material and with a 'wastage rate' of around 15 per cent that is of national concern. There are special stresses – social, academic and cultural – to which students are subject. These can erode a vulnerable, developing personality, provoke a latent psychosis or destroy an individual who cannot adapt.

However, there is every reason to suspect that the rate of breakdown among the non-student population in the same age group is roughly parallel (perhaps slightly less). The form of breakdown may not be so decisive and may not be so obviously apparent in a situation with less emphasis on consistently high performance, but it exists nevertheless and represents the type of adolescent disturbance which is the hardest to trace and treat.

It is in this group that the bulk of socially inadequate, unattached, drifting youth can be found. They are also the group who are most likely to be deeply involved in the drug sub-culture. The Simon Community's recent Report 406, *Yesterday's youth . . . today's tragedy*, contains the frightening figure that 52 per cent of the 406 people given emergency accommodation by the Community between December 1969 and May 1970 were aged between 15 and 25. The Report comments:

they have drifted into a world of drugs and alcohol and, in some cases, turned to crime to survive. Home to them is a back street doorway or a bench at Euston Station. In running away from their problems they have lost touch with society.

The Simon Community has always concerned itself with the 'social flotsam' which even other voluntary groups have shied away from. They have consistently tackled the 'drop outs' that are nearest the bottom of the barrel. The aim of other statutory and voluntary groups should be to catch these people, particularly the young, along the way before they have the chance to fall to the depths from which the Simon Community tries to lift them.

It is difficult to be optimistic in describing for parents the resources and facilities which exist to pick up and sort out adolescent emotional problems before they escalate into drug dependency or mental illness. There is some voluntary provision for youth consultation and referral (if necessary) throughout the country. Almost inevitably, of course, most of these services are in the south east. Clearly, the problems are not peculiar to London and the home counties, but services are inclined to mushroom in areas of greatest need. The south-east has become the area of greatest need simply because of the population drift, and the vicarious attraction of the capital with its anonymity and flourishing drug-scene. Both characteristics seem to act as a magnet not only for those bent on 'drop-out', but for the thousands of ordinary young people intent on proving their independence and 'doing their own thing'.

Some of the services, established originally by professionals in the fields of psychiatry and social work, have achieved very high reputations, chiefly because of their ability to offer guidance on their adolescent client's own terms. So London is fortunate in having the Brent Consultation Centre (Johnston House, 51 Winchester Avenue, London NW6), and the Tavistock Institute's advisory service (58 Belsize Lane, London NW3).

The greatest problem in setting up a consultation centre is simply getting young people to accept it and use it. Anything that smacks of 'establishment' and offers any hint of sermonising is doomed before it opens its doors. If the adolescents who would like advice have had 'generation gap' problems of communicating with their parents, it may take a long time for them to accept the idea that not all people of their parents' generation have closed minds or are intolerant and condemnatory.

Another danger is setting up a consultation centre that is inadequately staffed by experienced professionals (usually working on an evening sessional basis). Volunteers of the calibre of those working with the Samaritans, for example, are hard to find and need guidance and seminar tuition themselves before they can begin to be of value. A well-meaning but inexperienced volunteer can quickly get into very deep water when faced with a young person whose problem is simple *on the surface* but who may soon reveal himself to be deeply disturbed and in need of very careful handling.

None the less some young people's advisory services up and down the country offer a refuge and support to young people who otherwise might have nowhere to turn – no adults to whom they can at least confide their problems.

### Finding out about local sources of help

It would be impossible to give a comprehensive list of such services throughout the country. However it should not be too difficult to track down the consultation services that exist in your area. You can make a start with the telephone book. Check under 'Social service and welfare organisations' in the yellow pages. However, do not be disappointed if you draw blank, because the sort of advisory centre you are looking for does not always appear in this index.

Despite the rather unfortunate and persistent 'image' of local government, there are many local authority staff who are eminently approachable on this sort of matter. The Health Department will contain mental welfare officers and mental health social workers who will know of any consultation service. Many boroughs employ a youth group leader (he may go under various titles) to co-ordinate facilities and activities for young people: he would know of any rescue services for adolescents. So would the chief probation officer. Citizens' Advice Bureaux should have this kind of information at their finger tips. And the desk sergeant at the local police station is often an invaluable source of information – in any case some forces now have specialised youth liaison officers. If you draw a few blanks at first, *do* persist until you have explored all the possibilities.

If things do go seriously wrong in adolescence it is little use for the parents to try to deal with the problems entirely by themselves. For if it was a problem within their scope to solve, it would never have reached this acute level. It is better to hand over to someone who has the confidence of the adolescent. If you are lucky enough to have a well-developed service in your area, be sure to use it if a crisis should come.

*John Payne graduated in social studies and politics. He is assistant editor of 'Mental Health' and assistant public information officer of the National Association for Mental Health.*

# Advice to parents

## ALEXANDER MITCHELL

Since you are reading this booklet we can assume that as a parent you are concerned that your children might become involved in taking drugs, or at least that they may be at risk of doing so. Most people feel a responsibility and want to know what they can do to avoid this situation arising.

**1 – Should you be watching for signs that your children are misusing drugs?**
The answer is definitely 'No' for three reasons.

The first is a purely practical one. There are, in fact, no clear cut signs. Any evidence that a young person is misusing drugs can be confused with the natural disturbances of adolescence – the rapid shifts of mood, the dreamy preoccupation, the irritability, the restlessness and so on. An investigation in a new town showed that even among confirmed users there was a wide range of disagreement about definite signs of being 'on drugs'. There are a few unambiguous indications like the injection marks on the arms where heroin or barbiturates are being 'fixed', and a characteristic smell in the air when cannabis is being smoked. But these are so obvious that the young people make sure to keep them hidden.

The second reason is a matter of trust. Adolescence is a time when, despite how they behave or what they may say, young people need to feel that their parents trust them, and that they in turn can trust their parents. If the young people become aware of parental scrutiny, especially if it is surreptitious, they react in a hostile way. Trust has been broken, faith has been lost. Thus, the very point – trying to help – is frustrated and both sides lose even more ground.

The third reason is to do with expectancy. We react to others' expectations of us, and tend to behave in ways in which we imagine they believe we are going to behave. This is particularly true in conflict situations, especially when the expectation is critical or disapproving. The young person thinks 'Well, if that's how they expect me to behave, I'll damn well behave that way'. The unconscious aspect of this is that the young person can then blame the parents and largely disavow his responsibility in the action.

**2 – If you should not watch out for signs, what should you do?**
Communication and relationship are the key words. By the time our children have become adolescents we can no longer order them or bully them into doing what we want, or believe to be right. Adolescents correctly believe that they are persons in their own right and thus are entitled to decide for themselves what is right and what is wrong. In this situation we as adults have to relinquish our customary authoritarian attitude and be prepared to talk with young people in a relaxed, natural way. If we genuinely try to build an open relationship with them, they will respond and out of this reciprocal relationship will come communication. This must always pass in both directions, each respecting the individuality and autonomy of the other.

The way some people talk, you would think that adolescents belonged to some foreign race with whom it's impossible to communicate. This is only true if you make the mistake of being patronising and talking down to them, or what is worse taking up a rigid inflexible position of adult superiority. If communication is to take place round the subject of drugs there must be certain preconditions.

To start with parents need to be well informed about drugs of misuse – their nature and their true effects and damage. The biggest trap for us is to be found out by the young people because we make ill advised and unfounded generalisations, or inaccurate statements.

Despite popular belief, drugs are not the real subject of the debate – the misuse of drugs is only a symptom of a deeper malaise, the loss of personal identity or the rift between the generations. The discussion needs to range around all aspects of experience and not to concentrate on drugs alone. Young people urgently want to explore themselves and the environment around them. They are passionate about sex, politics, religion, personal philosophies and commitment to ideologies. These are the subjects to be talked about. Above all we will have to be prepared to reveal not only what we believe, but to reveal our deep personal selves.

None the less, as drugs often are the testing ground for finding out what the other believes, it becomes essential to declare what one's own attitude is, and openly to set limits for behaviour within the family. This allows the use of drugs to become 'socialised', as the use of alcohol has been socialised. So everyone knows where they are; there's no room for ambiguity, which leads to testing out or the unfair restrictions of new sanctions. Once more the setting of limits is not to be done in an autocratic way by the parents, but to be determined by mutual consent.

### 3 – What if after all this the young person is really in trouble?
Once it has been determined that a young person is misusing drugs I find that parents go through a number of reactions:

- stage of shock and disbelief – '*No, it can't be true.*'
- stage of numbness and hopelessness – '*It's no good, nothing can be done.*'
- stage of resentment – '*Why do you have to do this to us?*'
- stage of scapegoating – '*Someone's to blame and they should be made to pay for it.*'
- stage of denial – '*It hasn't really happened. He's only playing around with drugs.*'
- stage of rejection – '*Get out, I don't want to have anything to do with a person like you – junkie!*'

These are common human, emotional responses to deep hurt, and ultimately to a bereavement – the loss of a cherished ideal.

The trouble is that these emotional parental responses elicit equally emotional counter-responses in the young person:

- response of guilt – '*Now I know I really am wicked.*'
- response of resentment – '*What are they getting so steamed up for: it's all their fault anyway.*'
- response of rejection – '*I always knew they would let me down. Now I've only got my own crowd to rely on.*'
- response of despair – '*What the hell, it doesn't matter, I could be dead next week and who would care?*'

This is an unhelpful situation; it is a drawn battle – attack and counter attack in which each provokes the hostility and aggression of the other. But it is a normal human reaction: when we feel attacked, we attack back even if ultimately it draws more attack onto ourselves. Few people think the alternatives are feasible or desirable – flight from the attack, or submission. However, in emotionally-charged situations like this, appearing to give in, or being prepared to give in, or to accept the event for what it is, can often be the first step towards a reconciliation and forgiveness which are necessary prerequisites for conflict resolution and personal growth.

A great help in crisis situations like this are the old standbys:

- a cooling-off period
- keeping a sense of perspective
- if possible some sense of humour
- finally, knowing whom to turn to for help.

**Agencies who can be of help**
*The family doctor* is a natural person to turn to for help. He knows the family well and is on nobody's side. Thus he can be mediator between parents and the young person. He can deal with the medical aspects of danger to health, and control future supplies of the drug of dependence.
*The school medical officer* is in an important position in the school, which is where many young people first come into contact with drug misuse. He can again mediate between the school authorities, the parents and the pupil involved.
*Hospital treatment units* are available to provide both in-patient and out-patient facilities if the young person's health is in serious risk, and if he has become seriously dependent, either physically or psychologically.
*The probation officer* can work in conjunction with other social workers or medical specialists, both in the early pre-court case stage, or after prosecution. He provides one of many adult role models which the young person can use in building up a more secure and mature personality for himself.
*The police*, as well as being a law enforcement agency, are also concerned in reducing crime and in providing help for young people in trouble. They represent the real aspect of society's response to behaviour if it is deemed to be anti-social, or against the interests of the person involved.
*School teachers and headmasters* know an aspect of young people of which their parents are sometimes unaware: and they often have a relationship which is less traumatic because it has less emotional overtones. However, the headmaster may be in a difficult position if he has to choose between what is for the good of the individual pupil and what is good for the school as a whole.
*Associations for the Prevention of Addiction* are growing up in many towns and cities and are affiliated with the Association for the Prevention of Addiction (APA) of King Street, London, WC2. Such associations can provide a number of sorts of help: support groups for parents, factual information, details of whom to turn to in the local area, lectures, discussions, films and other ways of increasing awareness and responsibility. Some associations provide supporting discussion groups for the young people themselves and initiate counselling programmes.

Ultimately, the surest prevention must be based on each young person deciding that he will not use illegal drugs of dependence, because they are incompatible with his view of himself and with his own personal goals. The whole drugs issue provides a useful arena in which he can clarify his sense of personal responsibility.

In all of this, a parent remains the best person to support, guide and advise a young person. The parent, if only he can bring himself to admit it, has gone the same way before, and may not have made the same mistake, but has made mistakes of a similar kind, because it is inherent in human nature. All young people have to break away from parents and determine for themselves what kind of person they are going to become. The misuse of drugs is an unfortunate means of making this breakaway and determining self autonomy used by this current generation of young people.

*Dr Mitchell is consultant psychiatrist at Fulbourn and Addenbrooke's Hospitals in Cambridge. He is also responsible for the containment unit at Benet Place in Cambridge for the control of drug misuse. He is author of 'Drugs – the Parents' Dilemma' (Priory Press, 10s.).*

# Schools and drugs

## HARRY REE

*A lot of our problems arise because of the emotions still generated by the very word drug - Headmaster.*

Strong emotions were generated by a letter sent to the heads of 367 schools by the editor of WHERE last June. The sample included all recognised independent schools which had pupils over the age of 16 and where more than 50 per cent were boarders, and all direct grant grammar and state secondary schools which had at least 25 per cent boarders. The letter explained that ACE was investigating 'drug abuse among adolescents' including the risk of expulsion for involvement in a 'drug incident'. Each school was asked first what their policy was as far as expulsion for a drug incident was concerned, and secondly what their attitude would be towards accepting a pupil from another school 'who had been expelled for experimenting with cannabis'. Only two-fifths of the schools replied (139), but it was towards the end of the summer term, and those that did represented a very wide range of schools, including some of the Top Twenty, some well known denominational schools and a good proportion of run-of-the-mill private schools.

A recurring theme in the heads' letters was that it was impossible to give a blanket answer: each case would be considered on its merits. Almost all showed a real concern for this 'new problem', and for the 'erring' child who might be involved – this often included a recognition that any pupil expelled should be helped to obtain elsewhere the academic qualifications which he might have been expected to achieve in their school.

But very striking was the number of heads who revealed similar and stereotyped assumptions about drug takers; several assumed that pupils who experimented could be called 'addicts', that they had 'committed sins against the community', that they constituted 'a moral infection' in the school, such that 'quarantine might be necessary or sometimes an operation'. One head summed this up by indicating his conviction that they were a predictable type, since 'drug taking is a symptom of personality and behavioural defects which have shown themselves in other wrongs previously'.

The observation quoted at the beginning of this article was confirmed by nearly all the replies which showed that where drugs are concerned many heads are ruled by their hearts. But it must be stated that there may have been some confusion caused by the wording of the original ACE letter; this referred to 'drug abuse' in connection with the first question, and 'experimenting with cannabis' in the second. As long as cannabis is classed as one of the illegal drugs, it is perhaps understandable that schools should regard them all in the same light, but some heads seem to have allowed themselves to be carried away by the connotations of 'drug abuse', not only failing to distinguish between one drug and another, but even between taking the drug and possessing it. 'Pushing' (an emotive term they, like the rest of us, tend to use) was always regarded as being worse than either; otherwise a drug case was a drug case was a hard case.

Admittedly there are good reasons why many heads, most of them probably over 40, should find the problems presented by drugs in school exceptionally worrying. One is that it has been built up as the contemporary scourge, and the mass media have painted an almost totally black picture of the drug scene. But there is another reason why these heads could be expected to confront the problem with excessive caution, with fear and sometimes with excitement; this is simply because for them it is new. Several tried, in their replies, to make analogies between smoking reefers and smoking cigarettes or between drugs and homosexuality, between pushing hash and introducing drink to school. One head, for instance, confidently suggested that drug taking was 'a matter to be treated in exactly the same way as any other disciplinary problem, and that a boy who had been expelled from a school for misuse of drugs is in the same position as a boy who is being expelled for stealing, persistent indiscipline or for drinking'. Most however were more alarmist. For there is one vital difference between these 'expulsion crimes' and drug taking: the former were being practised when the heads were pupils, some of them may even have themselves indulged in them, 'in an occult manner', to use one head's phrase. In any case, they could the more easily understand and sympathise with these older forms of deviance – but the new one threw them. I found myself wondering if the future heads among their pupils would feel the same as these heads in 30 years' time – I doubt it.

Some, it is true (but a very few), showed a liberal approach; as so often with teachers, their own children had helped; one had a daughter who had told him that at university 'everyone experimented with pot'; another stated that he did not 'regard cannabis with the fear and horror which is the reaction of some adults, and I feel that there are many worse things in which adults as well as adolescents are involved'. But in general there was a lack of ability genuinely to feel with the new generation.

Even the kindly head who wrote that 'a girl taking drugs needed help, not condemnation' is perhaps failing to recognise that some of the pupils who will experiment with pot may not need the kind of help implied, and they could well be respectable, justifiably curious and responsible members of the community, on their way to win distinction for the school. Erich Goode has recently described such users in a *New Society* article (11 June 1970):

At the periphery of the marijuana scene is the experimenter, the extremely infrequent user, the dabbler. He has few marijuana smoking friends, is rarely presented with opportunities to try the drug, is curious about its effects but stops using it after curiosity is satisfied. *He may be the the most typical representative of all individuals who have ever used marijuana; at any rate he forms a sizeable minority of all users* (my italics).

Of course this does not rule out the others, the mixed up rebels and potential drop-outs who constitute the stereotype; of course, these need attention, but often this is exactly what they are seeking. One head in this connection drew the attention of ACE to an article by the psychiatrist Derek Miller, which noted: 'If the drug is used by adolescents inside a school, it is reasonable to assume that they have an unconscious desire to be caught'.

Of course this idea – that adolescents have an unconscious desire to be caught – is a difficult one for traditional heads to accept, but they do need to recognise its force, to recognise that young people who are out of sympathy with some of the overtly-expressed values and assumptions of the school, will actually want to be seen to rebel. And if this involves punishment, so much the better. One modern form of rebellion for the young – the fashionable way to protest, and arouse the hostility of those in authority – is clearly to be caught in a 'drug incident'.

The replies from schools show that there is a wide variation between the ones which seem not to have recognised this trend, and those which allow for it. One head with a reputation for liberal views wrote, with strange illogicality:

I have not yet had a case of a boy who had pot or smoked it at school whom I have not sacked . . . I believe that this policy is a means of protecting the school community . . . If this is a rule, the boys know where they stand, *and temptation is more or less removed from them* (my italics).

Among the expellers (and there were about 20 of these who were quite definite that expulsion would follow any discovered case) there was this tendency to erect an inflexible warning barrier, which was in some cases printed as a letter to parents. For example:

Your son may have told you that at the end of the term I spoke to the whole school about drugs . . . I think it may help if parents have a summary of what I said. (Five numbered points follow which include): experiment leads to tolerance, tolerance leads to addiction, addiction leads to physical and moral degradation. No healthy person needs drugs. Any suspected incident will be investigated, and the facts reported to the police. Anyone who is guilty of bringing drugs into the school or taking drugs while a member of the school will be expelled.

One headmistress wrote:

I have no scruples at all at letting it be known that instant expulsion will be the fate of anyone introducing drugs into the school. I am all for an ultimate deterrent even if I never mean to use it.

One feels that the experience of bringing up a family would have helped her here.

It is surprising that so many schools are prepared to tie their hands in this way, without realising that, by erecting prefabricated draconian punishments, they are constructing for some children a lure and a gin . . . which may be difficult to resist. For there is no doubt that, just as for each generation of teachers a particular misdemeanour takes on a special importance, so for children the same misdemeanour becomes fashionable, and many who want the limelight, as well as many who want to protest, are attracted like moths.

This fact is recognised by some schools: 'It is better not to batter away at the subject'. 'It appears to me unwise to give too much prominence to the dangers of drug abuse'. This attitude doesn't preclude occasional talks about it by 'sympathetic doctors' 'the superintendent of police' or 'Sister Patricia'.

One of the wary heads told how two of her parents, practising psychiatrists, had formerly visited schools to warn pupils of drug addiction, but:

They have now decided that their discussions merely titillated the students and encouraged experiment. Sadly enough one of their own daughters provided our first instance of the problem!

Several wisely recognised that while there might be no smoke without a fire, very often the 'smoke' arose from a very innocuous glow. Pride often entered into the business:

I would not recommend my Governors to expel a boy just because he had drugs on him, because these are, in all probability, carried only for bravado, in the same way that rather sad boys have, in the past, many years ago carried cigarettes, or more recently, contraceptives.

One head wrote:

Rumour was rife around the school that a certain group of boys were smoking pot and that one boy amongst them was pushing. When it was all investigated, including a police laboratory test to assure ourselves that our findings were correct, it turned out that the boy had bought a bag of mixed herbs at Sainsbury's and mixed them with tobacco to roll two cigarettes which he had sold to other boys for 10s each, claiming that they contained hash. There are many morals to this story!

In almost all cases there was a recognition that a decision involves a conflict, difficult to resolve, between succouring the individual and protecting the community – one head had noticed 'a wave of expulsions from schools' arising from drugs cases, and had been horrified at the inhumanity shown, but he admitted that even he might expel a boy if he thought this was in the interests of the majority of the pupils:

This consideration is a constant problem especially to head teachers in a Christian establishment, where one is reminded of the lost sheep principle from time to time.

On the other hand, the lost sheep principle did not worry some; one wrote that the case would probably involve a number of pupils, 'and the cabal set up in the school would incline me to decapitate at least the leader'. Others excused themselves by asserting that sheep lost through taking drugs needed specialist handling such as they 'and their overworked staff' could not be expected to provide.

But concern was not confined to the school community; not unnaturally parents had to be taken into consideration, and on two counts. First:

No parent would feel secure if it was known that such practices were allowed, or that the school was willing to take pupils who had been expelled from other schools for taking part in any form of drug taking.

Secondly:

Publicity is so damaging that those who, like myself and my Governors, sell education at a high price (fees £600) are very vulnerable to the scandal of a bad press or even of a whispering campaign.

These two points – moral responsibility to parents, and the danger of losing pupils and eventually livelihood, clearly counted for much, and explained the importance, already referred to, of 'keeping the matter entirely occult'.

Some heads made great play of judging the whole problem on the evidence, but like us all, they tended to listen to the evidence which confirmed their prejudices. One headmistress JP, for example:

The evidence seems to show that all hard drug takers inevitably start with cannabis, and once they have become addicted to cannabis it is a small step to carbon tetrachloride.

Another wrote:

We could pursue the evidence of the World Health Organisation or the research of the Ivy League American University which establish that quite small doses (of cannabis) can have lasting adverse effects on mathematical ability.

Both these favoured expulsion, but here is the other side:

As a JP, I heard a most erudite and comprehensive lecture by a Home Office pathologist . . . the point was stressed that whilst hard drugs are lethal and addictive, soft drugs were neither, and did not in themselves lead to hard drugs. This progression was in the character of the taker.

Many would discriminate with real sensitivity:

I have several boys in the school who have taken drugs (cannabis in most cases) at one time or another. I think it would have been monstrous to have expelled them, because the drug taking was occasional and experimental. We can help and they are quite willing to be helped. If, on the other hand, drug taking is part of a serious anti-social pattern in which a boy is openly rejecting us and any help we can give, the school may be doing more harm than good.

# WHERE reports on the replies from schools

Overall the request for information met an unenthusiastic response. Of the 367 schools contacted, over three fifths did not write back at all. Of the 139 heads who did reply just over a quarter were unwilling to give any indication whatever of their attitude to drug experimentation: three of these schools sent a bare acknowledgement; seven schools said they wished to make no comment; 17 schools said it depended on the circumstances; and 11 schools suggested some of the circumstances it would depend on.

The other 101 schools attempted to answer the two questions about their policy on expelling or accepting into the school a known experimenter with cannabis. The majority of these commented fully on the various factors which would determine their decision, and which would make it an individual one in each case. The rest said that they almost certainly would expel, or declared such an intention with no qualifications at all.

| | |
|---|---|
| **Number of schools basing decisions on individual cases** | **69** |
| **Number of schools certainly or almost certainly expelling** | **32** |

Thus a full third of the schools who trusted us with a long and frank account of their attitudes to drug-taking took a hard line.

The tone of the letters showed a certain variation. The first group, the majority, were neutral: they displayed unexceptional opinions, and were not detailed enough to reveal how well- or how ill-informed the writer was about drug-taking. A second group of replies was noticeably authoritative. These heads demonstrated a knowledge of the subject and a balance of judgement that was extremely encouraging. But a final group showed the reverse: their letters contained totally inaccurate statements, or prejudiced assumptions. The replies were distributed as follows:

| tone of replies | neutral | well-informed | ill-informed |
|---|---|---|---|
| **heads basing decisions on individual cases** | 51 | 15 | 3 |
| **heads expelling** | 21 | 1 | 10 |

Thus nearly one in three of the expelling heads displayed flaws in judgement, while only one in 17 of the more flexible heads did so.

The schools were not asked directly about the occurrence of drug-taking among pupils. However 63 schools volunteered this information: 26% had experienced drug-taking; 74% had not encountered the problem.

This is probably an unreliable guide to the incidence of drug-abuse in the schools taking part in our survey, however, since the expelling heads and the ones who declined to answer the questions were the least forthright on this particular point.

| | volunteering information % | not giving information % |
|---|---|---|
| **schools not answering questions** | 23 | 77 |
| **expelling schools** | 40 | 60 |
| **schools basing decisions on individual cases** | 60 | 40 |

And whereas any school might be happy to put it on record that no pupils had experimented with drugs, only a fairly self-confident school would like to admit to the reverse situation. We know that 12 per cent of all the schools writing to us had experienced drug-taking among pupils. A further 55 per cent omitted to mention that they were drug free. The actual level of experimentation is anyone's guess.

Others would be much more 'human' and less responsible in their discrimination:

If I found a child had brought cannabis into the school and it was a child who had not previously been in the running for being expelled for anything, and I like the child and get on well with her parents, I would have a long talk with them and the child, and hope to be able to forget about the incident. If on the other hand the child was a bit of a menace before the incident I would probably jump at the chance to 'pin something on her' and ask her parents to take her away.

This head added, no doubt thinking she was being considerate:

I do not see such a situation arising here before the fifth year so this would not really prejudice a child's chances very seriously, as she could always go to a crammer . . .

Some rely, perhaps with justification, on the good tone of the school to keep pupils out of trouble, others feel that religious sanctions are still powerful:

It is part of the religious instruction to teach girls responsibility towards their health and integrity as persons. Such teaching comes naturally with interest in the fifth commandment and St Paul's words calling on the early Christians to remember that they are temples of the holy spirit.

RE teachers in another school are involved in discussions about drugs, using the BMA family doctor booklets.

Not many referred to their legal duties, and this may be because reporting to the police would bring publicity; a few however welcomed the opportunity of turning the matter over to the police, who could be very discreet and provide a shock which might 'do the trick'. There seemed to be some confusion about whether a head would be liable if drugs were taken on the premises without his knowledge – perhaps the heads' associations should advise members about this and about their legal liabilities in general.

One fact emerged which will be of interest to parents. The type of school is no guide to the way they will react – often it was the high prestige schools which showed themselves to be most punitive and insecure – underlining the fact that their replies MUST be kept confidential. Others in the same category, feeling no doubt that they could discard from strength, took a liberal and confident line. Quaker and Roman Catholic schools were represented at both ends of the spectrum, as were the private schools. On the whole the state boarding schools recognised that they might have to 'contain' their problems – but the head even of one of these was in no doubt he would expel and report.

The whole exercise was surely worthwhile. One definite advantage accrues to ACE members – the organisation can now advise them wisely and in confidence about schools which might take children who have been expelled for taking drugs. Other parents too may feel, as a result of this survey, that the matter is certainly taken seriously in a very large number of schools, and that by careful questioning as prospective parents, it is possible to discriminate between those schools which would remain 'pure' at all costs (some parents may want this), and those which would temper the wind to the experimenting lamb.

There was one school which replied tersely to the ACE letter: 'The questions you ask cannot be answered by anyone with a sense of responsibility'. I think the large number of helpful, responsible, sensitive and revealing replies received by ACE have proved him completely wrong.

*Harry Ree is a former headmaster of Watford Grammar School. He is professor of education at York University, where he started the education department in 1961.*

# LEAs: policies and practices on drug education in schools

## SUE KEABLE

Do local education authorities consider themselves at all responsible for helping to prevent drug abuse among school children? In particular, do they feel it necessary to provide educative measures for the children in their areas? WHERE wrote to all principal and divisional school medical officers listed in the current *Education Committees Year Book* – 272 in all – to try and get some idea of what, if anything, is being done. We asked them if their authority provided day conferences on drugs for teachers or for pupils; material for teachers to use with classes or for their own information; or peripatetic teachers or health educators to provide teaching on drugs in schools. We also asked them to tell us about any other service they provided. We allowed three weeks for answers to come in, and during that time we received 124 replies. Eight of these were from small divisional executives who had passed on the letter to their county medical officer. That left 116 letters on which this article is based.

The letters reflect tremendously wide variations in policy – not only over *what* services authorities should be providing, but over whether they should be providing *any* services at all. An unqualified 'no' to all the questions we asked came, for example, from both Sunderland and Poole. On the other hand, Tynemouth, who aren't at the moment providing any services, felt that:

If it is evident as a result of your investigations that teaching about the dangers of drug-taking is becoming essential in schools then I think any help about appropriate films and publications you can give would be of value.

Other authorities added a word of explanation of their inaction: the service had 'never been requested by any teacher', or 'there is no drugs problem here'. Some of the authorities taking this stance argued that it was pointless to tell children the dangers of something they were not aware of: such a policy only gave an undue and unnecessary emphasis, and could arouse interest where there was none before.

I am rather of the opinion that there is no point in bringing to the notice of children a subject about which they appear to be indifferent – *Darlington*

Up to the present time no children in this area have become drug addicts and I feel that until this problem does arise in this area conferences and teaching on drug addiction would be likely to do more harm than good – *Radnorshire*

There seem to be three points which the 'no problem here' authorities have failed to take into account. First is the difficulty of knowing when a drugs problem is going to occur, so that an authority in all good faith may believe it is drug free, only to be shocked by contrary evidence. This was the experience of Gillingham:

Until very recently, frequent enquiries to the police have received the reply that drug-taking in the Medway Towns has been on a very small scale. However, the recent discovery that one

66

of our senior schoolboys had been smoking cannabis prompted further discussion with the police, when it was learnt that the Medway Towns had recently shot to the top of the local league in LSD and cannabis.

The second point is the usefulness of preventive measures. Assuming that an authority is quite correct in its assessment that drug abuse is minimal in the locality, it still has a choice between preparing pupils in advance of the problem appearing, or waiting until pupils have begun to experiment with drugs before taking action. If some authorities thought they saw a third alternative – doing nothing, since the problem would probably *never* appear, they ignored the third point.

This concerns the extent of an authority's responsibility for its pupils. Does it really extend only as far as its own boundaries? Or should health education take into account the likelihood that children will not live in the area for ever, and may need to be prepared in advance for the experiences that different environments will bring?

More young people than ever before are going to university or college after school – or are simply leaving home to work elsewhere. And, on the whole, they go to large cities where a drugs problem, on some scale, is more likely to exist. As Dr T. M. Cuthbert, president of the Royal Medico Psychological Association, told a meeting of Teesside sixth formers and students earlier this year:

It is just about as likely that a teenager will be offered soft drugs as it is that a girl will have a pass made at her before she is 20.

Since the young population is a mobile one, it is unreasonable to expect the drugs problem to stay in a handful of big cities: it's bound to spread. And as some young people move in towards the drug centres, so others move out, taking the habit with them. For example, Merioneth felt itself to be 'on the periphery of the drug problem' but was concerned about visitors coming into the town, bringing drugs with them. It now plans to arrange day conferences for head teachers. Carlisle exemplified the kind of authority that saw health education in this sort of context and accepted responsibility for preparing its youth for experiences beyond school, wherever they might be:

My own personal view is that the time has now come that all school children in fifth and sixth forms should be made aware of the dangers of drug abuse just as they are with other problems such as smoking and health, venereal disease, and so on. There is such an interchange of young people around the country after leaving school that while there is still no real problem locally these youngsters are bound to encounter it in other areas.

In fact, an official endorsement of the responsibility of local authorities to take part in drug abuse prevention work has already been given: in March this year the Advisory Committee on Drug Dependence commented in their report on *The Amphetamines and LSD*:

The preventive role that the schools can play is crucial, if only because the school is the one universal meeting-ground for all boys and girls between the ages of five and 15, and for substantial numbers in higher age groups. We were glad to learn that local education authorities and schools in increasing numbers are covering the risks of drug-taking in their normal health education programmes . . . we welcome the efforts which some local education authorities have made . . . by establishing or participating in joint working groups of all the agencies concerned, and we recognise the role played by the school doctor in acting as a link between the school and the local medical and welfare services.

So, given that education authorities ought to be doing something, what in fact is happening?

**Key to services referred to below:**

1 – providing written and/or visual materials

2 – holding or planning to hold day conferences for *pupils*

3 – holding or planning to hold conferences for *teachers*

4 – arranging lectures, talks or discussions for *pupils*, sometimes by health educators

5 – arranging lectures, talks or discussions for *teachers*

6 – including teaching on drugs in their health education syllabuses in schools

**Authorities providing all six services**

London (ILEA); North Riding (Yorkshire)

**Authorities providing five services**

Bradford (1, 3, 4, 5, 6); Glamorgan (1, 2, 3, 4, 5); Sutton London Borough (1, 2, 4, 5, 6)

**Authorities providing four services**

Birkenhead (1, 3, 4, 5); Brighton (1, 4, 5, 6); Bromley London Borough (1, 3, 4, 5); Colchester (1, 3, 4, 6); Croydon London Borough (1, 3, 4, 6); Cumberland (1, 3, 4, 6); Dewsbury (1, 4, 5, 6); Ealing London Borough (1, 4, 5, 6); Eastbourne (1, 3, 4, 6); Enfield London Borough (1, 3, 4, 5); Gloucester (1, 2, 4, 6); Kingston upon Hull (1, 3, 4, 6); Leeds (1, 2, 4, 6); Newcastle upon Tyne (1, 4, 5, 6); South Shields (1, 4, 5, 6); Suffolk (West) (1, 4, 5, 6); Sussex (East) (1, 4, 5, 6); Wolverhampton (1, 4, 5, 6); Worthing (1, 4, 5, 6)

**Authorities providing three services**

Bolton (1, 4, 6); Bournemouth (1, 4, 5); Bristol (1, 4, 5); Cambridgeshire and Isle of Ely (1, 4, 5); Canterbury (1, 2, 5); Cheltenham (2, 3, 4); Cheshire (2, 3,

---

The lists above give a breakdown on the kind of activities that are taking place up and down the country.

This picture, however, is likely to be changing all the time. Many authorities are in a state of flux about drug education, discarding old ideas for new ones. As one commented, the drug scene alters very quickly and methods of education need to be equally flexible. One way of keeping the whole question under review is to convene a panel of experts and relevant professionals to meet regularly: in fact 19 authorities either have set up or are setting up this sort of working party. At Doncaster, for example, the group is currently scrutinising the literature available. And the Halifax group has actually produced its own pamphlet telling parents how to detect and prevent drug abuse among their children – this is now distributed to all parents of secondary school children in the third, fourth and fifth years.

The distribution of booklets, tape recordings, films and other materials, or lists of sources of materials, does in fact represent the major effort being made by health education services in teaching about drugs: 79 said they did this. About a quarter of these use *About Drugs* by Dr J. D. Wright (Wolverhampton Health

6); Coventry (3, 4, 6); Flintshire (1, 4, 5); Gosport (1, 2, 3); Haringey London Borough (1, 5, 6); Harlow UDC (1, 4, 5); Havering London Borough (1, 3, 5); Hertfordshire (1, 4, 5); Ipswich (1, 4, 5); Lincolnshire (Holland) (1, 3, 6); Lincolnshire (Lindsey) (1, 3, 6); Liverpool (1, 5, 6); Oxford (1, 4, 5); Oxfordshire (3, 4, 6); Plymouth (1, 4, 6); Portsmouth (1, 4, 5); Redbridge London Borough (1, 3, 6); Shropshire (1, 4, 5); Sheffield (1, 4, 5); Southampton (1, 4, 6); Sussex (West) (1, 3, 6); West Riding Yorkshire (Rothwell/Wetherby) (1, 4, 5); Wigan (2, 3, 4); Worcester (1, 3, 4)

### Authorities providing two services
Bedfordshire (1, 3); Blackpool (1, 4); Cardiff (5, 6); Carlisle (1, 4); Chester (1, 6); Doncaster (1, 4); Dorset (1, 5); Durham (3, 6); Esher UDC (1, 4); Essex (4, 5); Gillingham (1, 4); Grimsby (1, 4); Halifax (1, 4); Harrow London Borough (1, 4); Hounslow London Borough (1, 6); Kent (1, 4); Lancashire (Clitheroe Division) (4, 5); Leicester (1, 6); Lincoln (1, 4); Monmouthshire (4, 5); Newcastle under Lyme (1, 4); Newham London Borough (1, 4); Newport (Mon.) (4, 5); Northumberland (1, 4); Reading (3, 4); Richmond upon Thames (London) (1, 6); Somerset (1, 3); Southport (1, 5); Staffordshire (4, 6); Stoke on Trent (1, 6); Swindon (4, 5); Teesside (2, 4); West Bromwich (1, 5); York (1, 4)

### Authorities providing one service
Barking London Borough (4); Exeter (4); Gloucestershire (4); Great Yarmouth (1); Isle of Wight (4); Lancashire (Accrington and Darwen Division) (5); Merioneth (3); Peterborough (6); Stockport (6); Suffolk (East) (4); Thurrock UDC (4); Wakefield (1); West Riding (Claro Division) (1); West Riding (Craven Division) (1); West Riding (Calder Division) (1); West Riding (Don Valley) (1); Woking UDC (3)

### Authorities providing no services
Barrow in Furness; Bootle; Bury; Darlington; Isle of Man; Poole; Radnorshire; Solihull; Sunderland; Tynemouth; Wallasey

Department, free to schools and youth clubs in Wolverhampton, 1s to others). Also quite popular were *Drug Dependence*, by Dr A. J. Wood (published jointly by the Corporation of Bristol and the Bristol Council of Social Service, 2s 6d); *Pot or Not*, again by Dr Wood (a Family Doctor booklet published by the British Medical Association, 1s 6d); and *Behind the Drug Scene* (another Family Doctor/BMA booklet, 2s). Some other titles were mentioned but were less widely used. These are clearly the key ingredients in current education on drugs. A parent could collect a batch of these pamphlets for less than 10s and gain quite a useful idea of basic work in schools. And the medical officers of health are on the whole quite satisfied with what literature is available. Those that are not raise this kind of objection:

So far it appears that very little material is available which can help with understanding the motivation towards drug-taking. The general line of education seems to be:

1 – Frighten the life out of the children
2 – Help parents to diagnose drug-taking in their own children
3 – Discard those who are addicted
4 – Never ask 'why?'                                           *—Gloucester*

I am afraid that my hopes have been frustrated by the lack of really satisfactory educational material; I would certainly welcome a better supply of any type of suitable material whether leaflets, more substantial publications or visual aids – *Colchester*

The wording in many of the standard handouts is far beyond the reading ability of the children
*–Dewsbury*

Films, however, were much more heavily criticised:

Many of the films are American in origin and show a very different cultural scene, so far as drug-taking is concerned, to anything seen in this country. Some of the films mention drug practices which are unknown to members of the audiences and it was felt unwise to show these films to young people, as they were likely to have interest stimulated – *Birkenhead*

Most of the films are either too extreme or horrific. Some, on the other hand, appear to make drugs too glamorous and attractive – *South Shields*

Too psychedelic and dramatic. The only British film, *The Addict Alone*, was long, tedious, and lacked action – *Worthing*

Most films are rather drab and do not hold the attention of restless teenagers – *Sutton*

There is not a single film which one would call a good teaching film, although some are useful for provoking discussions – *North Riding of Yorkshire*

The advice and information is usually given by elderly or middle-aged specialists, who, because of their age, represent the authority against which teenagers rebel – *Kingston upon Hull*

In despair of finding a good film, a doctor on the staff at the Wolverhampton Health Department – the author of the popular *About Drugs* booklet mentioned above – has himself written a script and is trying to obtain suitable finance for it. But the medical officer for three of the Lancashire divisions doubts whether films are a good idea anyway:

The very dramatic type of film probably has an immediate impact, but the long-term effect is probably less good because those viewing the films are inclined to dismiss them as being part of the fantasy world of television . . . Our general impression is that more effective results can be obtained by direct personal approach rather than by film or published material.

In fact many authorities relied on the personal contact of meetings, discussion groups and conferences to put the message across. Twelve authorities told us that they had held day conferences for pupils, though only a couple of these were *solely* on drugs. Usually they were on health education in general, with drugs taking a major part. More popular were lectures to children, held in 43 authorities, and/or talks given as part of their normal health education course – 41 authorities (some had both). In general authorities seemed to agree that day conferences were more useful if given for teachers, social workers and the like, so that one conference would have a much greater multiplying effect. Thirty-one authorities told us they had worked on these lines; and even more, 42, run shorter discussion meetings. Sheffield is a good example of a well-integrated programme:

We have a continuous programme of education about drug abuse for all levels of the population both lay and professional. In the early days of our campaign arrangements were made for some 1,500 professional workers including teachers, doctors, clergy, social workers, health visitors, police and others to attend conferences, seminars and film screenings on drug abuse and dependence. These are still undertaken as part of our on-going programme. We also co-operate with local and national professional organisations in the arrangement of conferences including the provision of speakers.

Not only was it more efficient to teach the teachers who could then teach the pupils, but large gatherings of school children could be unsatisfactory. For example, it wasn't always found to be a successful forum in which the pupils

70

could raise their own questions. This parallels the situation over sex education in schools. A good illustration is Michael Duane's story of a class discussion which sprang up over a father having beaten up his 14-year-old daughter because she was pregnant. He followed this by suggesting: 'Ask me any question you like and I will promise to answer it truthfully if I know the answer'. At this there were 'incredulous sniggers and muffled whispers', but no questions. He realised that 'they were afraid of the isolation demanded by asking a question', so he told them 'If you prefer you may write your question on paper and you needn't write your name. I will go out of the room for a few minutes. Put the papers on my desk before I return'. When he came back 'there was a pile of papers on the desk'.

Authorities frequently showed their appreciation that the situation must be right if discussion of many of the delicate issues in health education is to be successful. For some this argued against sending special health educators into schools:

It was felt in Ipswich that preventive action in schools depended on accurate and factual information being available to children but that there was a danger of creating an unhealthy interest in drugs if formal lectures were given by experts not normally associated with the schools
*– Ipswich*

I am opposed to large group education by outsiders on this topic and am concentrating on enabling teachers to deal with the subject spontaneously in the classroom context. However, this is supplemented by visits and discussions from health education staff. I will not undertake instruction on the subject of drugs out of the context of more general education – alcohol, cigarettes, relationships, sex and so on – *Haringey*

This reflects a view mentioned specifically by 15 other authorities: that drugs should *not* be treated in isolation, but as part of the whole health education spectrum.

It is not considered advisable to give health education on this one subject in isolation. It must be considered only as one aspect of an on-going dialogue in health education which covers the whole range of personal and social relationships – *Oxford*

The problem of drugs has come to stay and may well get worse. It should not be considered in isolation but should be taught in school as part of a comprehensive scheme of health education – *Worcester*

It's difficult to draw any broad conclusions from these letters: after all, only 42 per cent of the authorities replied. Of course we'd like to know what the other 58 per cent are doing: one might be forgiven for thinking that they're perhaps doing nothing but are unwilling to admit it. But this sort of speculation may be unfair. Still, what does seem clear is that some authorities have a carefully thought-out, well-planned policy on drug education for their pupils: others have not. The replies we received reveal almost a hotch-potch of confusion: with the fear of creating an interest, and thereby a problem, lurking in many a medical officer's mind. 'Teachers will wish to give pupils the kind of help which might prevent drug-taking' says the Department of Education and Science's *A Handbook of Health Education*. Well, the teachers might wish to, but they can't always be sure of getting any sort of help from their education authorities.

*Sue Keable has been assistant editor of WHERE for four years, and has written on various topics including immigrants at school, women in the professions, teacher training for mature students and Common Entrance. She was one of the contributors to the* Sunday Times *'A to Z on education'.*

# Where to find out more

## 1 – About the drugs themselves

*All About Drugs*, Franz Bergel and D. R. A. Davies, Nelson, 42s.

*Amphetamines, Barbiturates, LSD and Cannabis*, Report No 124, Department of Health and Social Security, HMSO, 7s 6d.

*Drug Addiction*, Office of Health Economics, 2s 6d.

*Drugs from A-Z*, Richard Lingeman, Allen Lane, The Penguin Press, 50s.

## 2 – About drugs and the law

*Drugs and Civil Liberties*, National Council for Civil Liberties, 5s.

*Drugs and the Police*, Terence Jones, Butterworths, 10s.

*Release Report on Drug Offenders and the Law*, Sphere Books, 5s.

## 3 – About controversies over drugs

*Drugs*, Peter Laurie, Penguin, 5s.

*Social Problems of Drug Abuse*, Frank Dawtry, Butterworths, 15s.

*Aspects of Drug Addiction*, Martin Silberman, Royal London Prisoners Aid Society, 56 Stamford Street, London SE1, 7s 6d.

## 4 – About those who take drugs

*Drugs and Schoolchildren*, R. S. P. Wiener, Longman, 50s.

*Turn me on, man*, Alan Bestie, Tandem, 5s.

*The Addict in the Street*, Jeremy Larner and Ralph Tefferteller, Penguin, 4s 6d.

*The Drug Scene in Great Britain*, M. M. Glatt *et al.*, Arnold, 15s.

*The Drug Subculture: a Christian Analysis*, Kenneth Leech, Church Information Office, 2s.

## 5 – Material for young people on drugs

*About Drugs*, J. D. Wright, Health Department, 59 Waterloo Road, Wolverhampton, 1s.

*Connexions: Out of your Mind?*, Peter Newmark, Penguin Education, 5s.

*Pot or Not?*, A. J. Wood, BMA, 1s 6d.

*Behind the Drug Scene*, BMA, 1s 6d.

*Drugs for Young People: their Use and Misuse*, Kenneth Leech and Brenda Jordan, Religious Education Press, 10s 6d.

## 6 – other books or booklets for parents

*The Willing Victim: a Parents' Guide to Drug Abuse*, G. Birdwood, Secker and Warburg, 35s.

*Drugs: the Parents' Dilemma*, A. R. K. Mitchell, Priory Press, 10s.

*Drug Dependence*, Antony Wood, Corporation of Bristol and Bristol Council of Social Service (Health Department, Tower Hill, Bristol 2), 2s 6d.

*The Age Between*, Derek Miller, Cornmarket/Hutchinson, 10s.

# Some useful addresses

*Association for the Prevention of Addiction* and *Association of Parents of Addicts*, both at 16 King Street, London WC2.

*Chelsea Addiction and Research Centre*, 88 Beaufort Street, London SW3.

*National Association for Mental Health*, 39 Queen Anne Street, London W1.

*National Association of Probation Officers*, 6 Endsleigh Street, London WC1.

*Youth Service Information Centre*, National College for the Training of Youth Leaders, Humberstone Drive, Leicester, LE5 ORG.

*National Council for Social Service*, 26 Bedford Square, London WC1.

*National Council for Civil Liberties*, 152 Camden High Street, London NW1.

*Release*, 50a Princedale Road, London W11.

*Institute for the Study of Drug Dependence*, Chandos House, 2 Queen Anne Street, London W1M OBR, which can also direct parents to further sources of information and help.

# Sources of teaching materials on drug addiction

*Camera Talks Ltd.*, 31 North Row, London W1.

*Concordia Films*, 177/123 Golden Lane, London EC1.

*Boulton Hawker Films Ltd.*, Hadleigh, Ipswich, Suffolk.

*British Temperance Society*, Stanford Park, Watford, Herts.

*Sound-Services Ltd.*, Kingston Road, Merton Park, London SW19.

*Foundation Film Library*, Brooklands House, Weybridge, Surrey.

*Medical Recording Service and Sound Library*, Royal College of General Practitioners, Kitts Croft, Writtle, Chelmsford, Essex.

*Health Education Council Ltd.*, Tavistock House North, Tavistock Square, London WC1.

*Concord Films Council*, Nacton, Ipswich, Suffolk.

*Church of England Council for Social Aid*, Church Information Office, Deans Yard, London SW1.

*Encyclopaedia Brittanica International Ltd.*, Dorland House, 18–20 Regent Street, London SW1.

*Diana Wyllie Ltd.*, 3 Park Road, Baker Street, London NW1.

*Carwal Audio Visual Aids*, 250 Woodcote Road, Wallington, Surrey.

# ABOUT ACE

## founded
- in 1960 as an independent, non-political, non-profit-making body

## aims
- to provide advice and information on education for parents
- to stimulate the setting up of new sources of help for parents
- to encourage closer home-school relationships
- to arouse informed discussions on educational issues
- to press for greater consideration of the parent's viewpoint in educational thinking

## methods
- WHERE, a subscription magazine on education for parents and for all concerned in education
- *Advisory Service* offering help with specific educational problems
- *Research and Action* projects designed to investigate areas of need and to demonstrate possible solutions

## membership
- ACE has 23,000 members who also receive WHERE for an annual subscription. If you are concerned with education – as a parent, teacher, student or administrator – you will be interested to read WHERE
- Send for subscription details to
  Richard Blake,
  Advisory Centre for Education,
  32 Trumpington Street,
  Cambridge CB2 1QY.